*The Bible and the
Moral Life*

The Bible and the Moral Life

C. FREEMAN SLEEPER

WESTMINSTER/JOHN KNOX PRESS
Louisville, Kentucky

For My Children
Paul and Mark
Deborah and Jonathan

*a small offering in return
for all they have meant to me*

Scripture quotations from the New Revised Standard Version of the Bible are copyright © 1989 by the Division of Christian Education of the National Council of the Churches of Christ in the U.S.A., and are used by permission.

Book design by Publishers' WorkGroup

First edition

Published by Westminster/John Knox Press
Louisville, Kentucky

This book is printed on acid-free paper that meets the American National Standards Institute Z39.48 standard. ∞

PRINTED IN THE UNITED STATES OF AMERICA

2 4 6 8 9 7 5 3 1

Library of Congress Cataloging-in-Publication Data

Sleeper, C. Freeman (Charles Freeman)
  The Bible and the moral life / C. Freeman Sleeper. — 1st ed.
       p.   cm.
  Includes bibliographical references.
  ISBN 0-664-25375-X (alk. paper)

  1. Ethics in the Bible.   2. Christian ethics—Biblical teaching.
3. Church and social problems.   I. Title.
BS680.E84S488 1992
241—dc20   91-45747

Contents

Preface

This book has a double focus: on biblical ethics and also on the use of the Bible in Christian ethics. It has been in process for several years in many different formats: talks, sermons, adult Bible classes, papers at professional meetings, and some of my courses. During that time, I have learned something from the comments and criticisms of too many people to name here.

I hope that the book will be useful in adult study courses. The "exercises" throughout the book are designed to do two things. If you are reading the book by yourself, they should help you to wrestle with the biblical texts and relate them to your own life. If you are part of a group, the questions should help to stimulate discussion. In a study class of thirteen weeks (one-quarter of the church school year), you might want to divide chapter 1 into three units and spend a week on each one. Chapter 2 could easily become two units (one on the Old Testament, one on Paul and the rest of the New Testament) or even three. On the other hand, some groups may want to skip the preliminary material in chapter 1 and move directly to a study of the biblical sources. Also, chapter 8 is long enough that it can easily be divided into two or three parts. Or, you may want to focus on just one or two of the sections. Each section stands pretty much on its own.

In part 1, in order to make comparisons easier, I have used basically the same outline in each section. The first part describes the *context* or setting of the material. I have tried not to let this section become too long, but to give you just enough introduction so that you can get more out of your reading of the biblical passages. I have tried to define terms that may not be familiar to all readers of the book. The next part looks at the *content* of each writer or book: issues, themes, and advice. The third part examines the *arguments* an author uses to support that content. In technical terms, these are the "backings" or "warrants" or "appeals" that an author uses to defend a position; I have used the term argument because it is less confusing. Finally, I try to look at the *authority* the authors claim for themselves and/or their messages.

Biblical quotations are from the New Revised Standard Version. In referring to biblical dates, I have used "B.C.E." ("before the common era") and "C.E." ("common era"), since the Hebrew Scriptures are part of our common heritage.

I want to thank Roanoke College for the time to work on this book. I was the resident coordinator of a Washington Semester of the Lutheran College Washington Consortium during the spring of 1990, which gave me access to library resources in the District of Columbia. Then followed a sabbatical leave during the fall term of 1990, when the first draft of this book was written. During that year I was also a visiting scholar at the Churches' Center for Theology and Public Policy in Washington. I am grateful to Dr. James Nash, the executive director, for that opportunity. The libraries at Roanoke College, Wesley Theological Seminary, and Wake Forest University met my research needs; my thanks to the staff of those libraries who helped me when I needed it. My colleagues at Roanoke have helped me with the thought process, and also by not interfering when I was busy typing.

Parts of chapters 7–9 appeared in a very different form in *Theology and Public Policy* 2 (1990), published by the Churches' Center for Theology and Public Policy, and are used here by permission. Also, permission has been granted by Graded Press to use the long description of the "just war" theory from *In Defense of Creation*, the statement by the United Methodist Council of Bishops (1986).

Carla Barnes read and edited an earlier version of this manuscript when she was an undergraduate. Her fearless criticism has kept me from making many blunders. I am perfectly willing to take responsibility for the ones that remain. Also, my colleagues Robert Benne and Ned Wisnefske read portions of the manuscript and offered helpful advice.

This book really has a dual purpose. On the one hand, it presents an alternative to a literal or fundamentalist way of reading the Bible. I am not trying to present this alternative in a hostile way, since I have been impressed by the sincere and confident piety of many who read the Bible from that point of view. On the other hand, I am distressed by the widespread ignorance of the Bible in our culture. I am convinced that the message of the Bible is still relevant, but only if we can express it in a way that deals with the complexity of the problems we face. Whether I have done that or not, you as the reader must decide.

1

Using the Bible: Getting Started

We have choices to make all the time. Some are trivial or mundane practical matters, while others have serious moral implications. For example, a stranger approaches you on the street and asks you to contribute to a fund for the widow of the Unknown Soldier. A celebrity whom you admire asks you on TV to buy a particular make of car. A candidate for public office asks for your vote solely on the basis of his or her stand on the abortion issue.

Many books on the Christian moral life deal with such issues at a strictly personal level. This book is not one of them. Rather, the focus here is on the way in which groups of Christians have used the Bible when they take a position on complex social issues. Indirectly, however, the book should help you to see the Bible as a resource in your own wrestling with moral issues.

For hundreds of years, the Bible has inspired and guided both Christians and non-Christians. Within the church, Christians have given the Bible a special or even an exclusive status as a guide to the moral life. Yet, in practice, believers have reached very different conclusions about the kind of behavior that is required.

Many have wondered, "Why do church bodies, each claiming to take Scripture as an authority, reach such different conclusions about the moral life?" In the following pages, we will try to find some answers to that question.

In this first chapter, we need to deal with some preliminary questions. One of the reasons why we as Christians reach different conclusions is that we start with different assumptions: about the authority of the Bible (why it should be read), about the proper way to interpret it (how it should be read), and about its role in shaping the moral life.

The headings in this chapter are deliberately open ended. On the one hand, my first task is to *describe* the way in which people have read and used the Bible. By doing nothing more than that, I would be following the advice a lovely woman once gave to me: "All you have to do in the church is just please everybody." On the other hand, I also want to say something about the way in which we *should* read the Bible. I believe that some ways of reading Scripture are better than others, and you should know in advance what my approach is.

WHY READ THE BIBLE?

There are many people who don't know, or don't care, what the Bible has to say. They may have been brought up in an environment where it was never mentioned. They may share the values of our secular culture, in which biblical religion is seen as superstitious and outmoded. Others may have been brought up in a strict, pietistic setting and have rejected the Bible in favor of popular psychology or contemporary literature. If you are one of those people, I hope you will continue reading and will discover that the Bible can be an important source of moral insight. It is much more likely, however, that you already share the conviction that the Bible is important.

Exercise 1

Before you read any farther, suppose that you are leading a Sunday school class of junior high school students. One of them asks you,

Using the Bible: Getting Started

"Why should we read the Bible, anyway?" Take time now to write down the answers you might give to that student. If you are one of a group of people reading this book, take time to discuss your answers with each other.

If you are like most people, you would probably give several kinds of answers to the question "Why read the Bible?" Some of them are what we might call "functional." You may have claimed that the Bible "works." It has made a difference in your life, or it has the power to change the life of a teenager. Other answers probably imply that the Bible reveals God's purpose. It is "the Word of God," or it is a collection of writings "inspired" by God. All of these are "truth claims" of different sorts. The first type of argument is common in the social sciences. If the Bible can transform a person's life, that is an important fact, even if there really is no God, and even if the Bible is only the product of the human imagination. This approach appeals to the American preference for what works, for what produces results, for "the bottom line." The second type of argument appeals to what is "real," whether or not it is practical. The message of Scripture is to be faithful to God's purpose for human life, at whatever cost. Faithfulness to God is what counts, not human success.

We will consider four positions, without pretending that they exhaust all the possibilities (see table 1.1).

TABLE 1.1
Arguments for Biblical Authority

Based on Function		Based on Revealed Truth	
1. Cultural literacy	2. Personal satisfaction	3. Meaning of life	4. Verbal inerrancy

Cultural Literacy

In an adult class in which we did exercise 1, someone immediately mentioned the argument I have called "cultural literacy."

We should read the Bible, this person said, so that we will be able to understand our Western heritage. If we do not know the Bible, we will not be able to understand the symbols in much of our great literature and art and music. To be an educated person, we need to study the Bible.

In my years of teaching biblical courses, I am constantly amazed by what students do not know. Some of the answers are humorous by accident (I hope), such as the student who wrote, "Jesus was born in a manger," or the one who said, "God created the world in six days, and made Adam and Eve have Jesus without making love." Other answers are more puzzling. One student thought that Jesus, after his baptism, went into the forest for forty days and nights. Another, who failed an exam, was heard complaining that his grade wasn't fair; he knew that the four Gospels were written by Matthew, Mark, Luke, and Moses.

For the past several years, I have given a "literacy test" during the first class session of each term. Students answer the questions anonymously. Their answers help me to know what kind of background they have, so I can pitch the course to their level of understanding. Then, during the term, I use a "literacy guide" identifying key passages, so the students will at least be able to recognize and locate them. (You will find the "literacy test" for the New Testament at the end of this chapter. If you want to test your own knowledge, see if you can answer the questions.)

Not more than 5 percent of my students can answer all the questions correctly at the beginning of the term. In part, this lack of cultural literacy may reflect the failure of the churches to educate. To a greater extent, it reflects the growing secularization of our culture. In either case, it seems to be a compelling reason to include more study of "the Bible as literature" within the public school curriculum. It is certainly one good argument for the importance of the Bible.

This is, however, a "functional" argument. It makes no claims that the Bible is "true" or that it is more important than other literature. It simply says that we need to know more about the Bible if we want to understand our own history and culture.

Personal Satisfaction

Related to that first argument, but at a more personal level, is what I have called "personal satisfaction." People who use the Bible regularly as part of their devotional life often find there is something missing when they neglect it for a time. This kind of devotional study provides a sense of comfort, of security, and of direction. It is a kind of spiritual "cookbook" or "auto mechanic's manual," to use two analogies offered by members of that same adult class.

The reason why I have treated this as a "functional" argument is that it focuses on individual needs. If you feel that the Bible makes sense for you personally, that it satisfies all of your spiritual longings and desires, that is an important claim. However, while you may feel that this book provides the clue to your own life, you may doubt that it would be equally convincing to someone living in another culture shaped by different sacred writings. Are you willing to argue that their Scripture is false and yours alone is true? If not, then you have really accepted the functionalist position. Or perhaps you feel that the Bible is important in your spiritual life, but that science really has all the important answers about the way in which the world actually operates. If so, you have adopted the functionalist position.

Meaning of Life

The third position is quite similar to one just described, but it differs in claiming that the Bible reveals the truth about the human condition. More than any other historical document, it discloses the meaning of human life. It is true not just because it makes sense to you and me, but because it explains the deeper truth of every historical period, every human culture, and even of the cosmic order.

It is almost impossible to illustrate this point of view in a brief space, so let me give just one example of a contemporary interpretation of the biblical message for our own culture.

During the 1950s and 1960s, there was a popular effort to recover a "biblical theology" in terms of the concept of "salvation history." One good example of this approach is *The Book of the Acts of God*, a collaborative venture by G. Ernest Wright and Reginald H. Fuller, Old and New Testament scholars, respectively. They identify a unique view of history in the Bible. In the Old Testament, this is expressed in a series of "recitals" of what God has done for Israel; these recitals serve as confessional statements. "There are, then, five 'events' in the Old Testament in which the whole faith seems to centre. These are the call of the fathers, the deliverance from slavery, the Sinai covenant, the conquest of Canaan, and the Davidic government."[1]

Similarly, in the New Testament, the faith of the early church is expressed in the "kerygma" or preaching, which gives voice to their experience of what God had done for them.

> In the New Testament story the following appear to be the important events: (1) The real life and teaching of Jesus. (2) His death on a cross at the hands of the Romans. (3) His resurrection as head of the new community established in him, that is, the Church.[2]

Both Testaments describe the way in which God relates to the social order and even to nature, based on this conviction that God is active in historical events.

Notice what this position does and does not claim. It claims that God is uniquely revealed in the historical experience of the biblical community. However, it does not claim that the Bible is infallible. There may be historical inaccuracies. The record of some events, such as the miracle stories reported in the Gospels, may have been shaped and even distorted by the biblical writers. There may even be contradictory evidence, such as the accounts of the conquest of Canaan in Joshua and Judges, or the question whether Jesus died on the day of Passover or during the day of preparation for that meal. None of these details, however, discredit in any way the biblical claim that God is disclosed uniquely in the historical experience of the covenant people, and particularly in the Christ event.

Verbal Inerrancy

For many Christians, however, it is not enough to claim that the Bible reveals the meaning of human life. It must be accepted as true in every respect. This claim is known as verbal inerrancy, although the terms "infallibility" and "plenary inspiration" are often used as equivalents.[3] In the United States, these terms have been used by a variety of evangelical Christian groups, but they have been most closely identified with the movement known as Fundamentalism, which received its name from a series of twelve volumes published between 1910 and 1915 by two wealthy brothers, Lyman and Milton Stewart of California. The movement had an intellectual leader in J. Gresham Machen, who left Princeton in 1929 to found Westminster Seminary, and who also helped to found the Presbyterian Church in America in 1936.

At least three strong motivating factors have characterized this movement: a rejection of the "biblical criticism" that developed during the nineteenth century and that we shall examine in the next section of this chapter; a rejection of modern science, particularly in the form of Darwinism and the theory of evolution; and a strong concern with a decline in the church's influence on public morality. To put the matter in a more positive way, the movement has developed its own agenda: a style of biblical interpretation based on the assumption of the "plenary inspiration" of Scripture, an interpretation of the natural world called "creation science" or "scientific creationism," and a variety of efforts to identify America as a "Christian nation." These efforts include the insertion of the words "under God" in the Pledge of Allegiance, demands for prayer in the public schools, and support for "right to life" legislation.

In recent years, the struggle over verbal inerrancy has been most apparent within the Southern Baptist Convention, where it has taken on political dimensions in a struggle for control of the seminaries and therefore of access to the ministry. Other

7

denominations have faced similar internal struggles over the proper understanding of biblical authority. For example, at its annual General Assembly meeting in June 1991, the Presbyterian Church (U.S.A.) overwhelmingly rejected the report of a task force on "human sexuality," in large part because the report was itself seen as a rejection of "biblical morality" or of a "biblical view of sex and marriage."

To an unusual extent, in the mass media the Fundamentalist position is identified as "the biblical view," so that a literal interpretation of the Bible is often presented as the only viable one. Many people, including church members, draw the conclusion that they either have to accept the Bible literally or throw it out the window.

In what follows, it will be clear that I do not accept the claim for verbal inerrancy, for several reasons. First, by denying the possibility of human error or of human influence on the text, this position is not really incarnational. A church which claims that Christ was both human and divine should not deny the humanity of the biblical record. If we take that humanity seriously, then we must assume that the Bible had its own literary development, and to understand it we must be free to study the Bible as we would other documents. Second, while many biblical characters do claim God's authority for their message, they do not claim infallibility; and if they did, we probably would not trust them. Even when a special effort is made to underline the credibility of a biblical writer (for example, in Deuteronomy 1:1 or John 21:24 or 2 Peter 3:15–16), the words are not those of the original speaker or author. Third, we have to remember that in the case of both testaments, there was a long period of time in which the messages were passed on by word of mouth before they were written down. Even in a culture that values this kind of oral tradition, the chances are that the tradition will be remembered and passed on in different forms. Indeed, when the words were written down, they were often dictated, as we can see in the case of Jeremiah (36:27–32) and Paul's letters. This process opens up the possibility of scribal error.

Instead, my position will fall most clearly into the category I have called "the meaning of life" argument. I do believe that the Bible tells the truth. It speaks about a universe and a history that depend upon a gracious God. It says that as human beings we inevitably destroy the relationships God intends us to have with God, with each other, and with the natural order. But it also speaks about the way in which that same God has acted to restore those relationships. This promise of fulfillment is intended for all human beings. This biblical message, I believe, tells things the way they really are. At the same time, we can feel free to use the functional arguments we looked at earlier. Once we are familiar with the biblical message, we are more likely to be grasped by its truth.

HOW TO READ THE BIBLE

Just as claims about the authority of Scripture differ, so there are many ways to interpret the biblical texts. On the one hand, if you assume verbal inerrancy, then you will look for ways of reconciling differences between accounts when they occur. You will also look for evidence to support traditional claims to the authorship of the biblical books. On the other hand, if you assume that collectors and editors and authors left their own imprint on the biblical writings, then you will want to use techniques of interpretation that have proven useful in other disciplines. In fact, biblical scholars are notorious borrowers of methods from literature and history and the social sciences. In some cases, the things we need to know in order to understand these ancient texts are quite technical, so we must rely on the work of experts. Textual critics, for example, try to establish the oldest and most reliable text. They try to come as close as possible to the original words of Isaiah or Paul. In order to do this, they need a command of ancient Near Eastern languages that most of us do not have, plus access to copies of the oldest biblical documents. Archaeology is another discipline that can shed light upon the biblical world, but it also requires a commitment of time and money and study that most amateurs cannot afford.

In other ways, however, most biblical interpretation is like trying to solve a murder mystery. If you know how to look for clues, and if you know how to ask the right questions, you can begin to unravel the meaning of even the most difficult passages. Other people may approach the task with more sophisticated equipment, but you can begin with the tools you already have. Even though the work of scholars can help you, you too can be a detective.

Exercise 2

Before we look at different ways of interpreting Scripture, take a passage that is familiar to you: Psalm 23, or the Beatitudes in Matthew 5, or Paul's "hymn to love" in 1 Corinthians 13. Make a list of all the questions you would have to ask if you really wanted to understand that passage. If you are in a group, discuss your answer with one another. If other questions occur, write them down. Keep them all in mind as you read this next section.

We cannot consider all of the relevant approaches, so I will try to group them into three major categories. If you want to know more about any of them, almost any introduction or survey or standard textbook will have a section explaining these approaches in more detail.

Reconstruct the Past

One approach to the Bible is to *reconstruct the past.* You would be doing that if you wanted to know "Who wrote this psalm?" or "How was it used?" You would be doing that if you asked, "Were these Beatitudes original with Jesus?" and "What did he mean by 'Kingdom of Heaven'? Is that the same as 'Kingdom of God'?" You would also be doing that if you asked, "Who were the Corinthians?" or "What did Paul mean by 'love'?"

This approach used to be called "higher criticism," in contrast to a "lower" or what we have called "textual" criticism. More often it is described as "historical criticism" (since it uses all the tools historians use to interpret the past) or as "literary-historical criticism" (since it includes tracing the development of the biblical literature). At its most basic level, the focus of the approach is to answer five questions, which I call the "five *w*'s": who, to whom, when, where, and why. In using this approach, you would want to discover as much as possible about the author, about the audience, about the time and place and circumstances when the documents were written, and especially about the author's purpose in writing. In order to determine this last point, we need to know something about the author's style, the meaning of key terms, and the structure of the argument, as well as any stated (or implied) intention.

There have been periodic shifts of emphasis within this effort to reconstruct the history of Israel, of early Christianity, and of their respective literary records. An early effort, using the tools of literary criticism, was to identify different strands or sources. Then, with the recognition that much of the biblical literature rested on earlier oral traditions, scholars attempted to identify the preliterary development: different "forms" and their "settings in life," that is, their function within the community. This approach, generally referred to as "form criticism," made use of the anthropological tools used to study the legends and myths of other cultures. However, as this approach led to a focus on smaller and smaller units, such as individual psalms or isolated sayings of Jesus, people began to feel that they were losing the larger picture. As a result, the focus began to shift again, this time to focus on the way in which biblical "authors" (or editors or redactors) took the materials available to them and wove them into a consistent narrative. This approach was therefore usually called "redaction criticism." More recently, scholars have shown an interest in using the techniques and concepts of the social sciences, particularly anthropology and sociology, to gain a deeper understanding of the social structure of the various communities that existed during the biblical history.

We simply cannot afford to sweep aside these efforts to reconstruct the past; their benefits are too important. For one thing, they help us to guard against reading our own ideas into the Bible. They force us to recognize that even when they use the same language, biblical writers do not necessarily mean the same thing. We must ask what words meant in their original context. In the second place, these efforts make us aware that the Bible did not descend directly from heaven. Rather, it took place in a world context that was very different from our own. By looking at that world—for example, creation stories and wisdom sayings in the ancient Near East, or the sayings of rabbis who were contemporaries of Jesus and Paul—we can gain a new appreciation for the way in which the Bible was like those other cultures and how it differed from them.

At the same time, there are at least two dangers in this approach. The first is *irrelevance*. Reconstructing the past becomes an end in itself, a task reserved just for specialists. Then the Bible is so far removed from our own world that it becomes an antique, something to be admired but not used. When that happens, the Bible loses its power to speak to us directly and to shape our lives. It loses its power to challenge and transform our ideas, our wills, our behavior. A second danger is *paralysis*. To be perfectly honest, while scholars have reached a consensus on many historical questions, other issues are far from resolved. Sometimes the evidence that we have is just too fragmentary. Other issues, like the use of the strange title "Son of Man" for Jesus in the Gospels, have divided scholars so badly that no consensus seems possible.

In the pages that follow, then, I will accept these efforts to reconstruct the past. However, I will use this approach as one stage in our search for the meaning of the biblical message, and not as an end in itself.

Creating a Dialogue

Partly in response to the dangers just mentioned, another approach has developed in recent years, which I would call *creating a dialogue* with the texts. Biblical interpretation, especially as it applies to the Christian moral life, should ideally take place in three stages.[4] The first step is to clarify our perspective or "how we see." The second examines "what we see" when we look at the Bible, especially by examining ethical themes in the biblical sources. The final stage involves "how we express what we see." That is, we need to communicate the results of our biblical study, to relate them to the moral issues that concern us. In addition, the last stage may involve a dialogue at several levels: between biblical images and contemporary secular images; between biblical images and contemporary models, such as those in the social sciences; and between biblical images and contemporary ethical theory. Therefore, in this opening chapter, we are examining our perspective, our assumptions. Then part 1 will examine four styles of ethical reflection within the Bible. Part 2 will explore the way in which church bodies have used Scripture in explaining their positions on social policy.

Liberation theology uses a similar approach. Particularly in Latin America, Christians in base communities gather to read and understand the Bible. They begin by examining their own situation. In common with many women and blacks in our own country, they understand their situation to be one of oppression. The first stage of biblical study, then, is to talk about specific incidents in their own lives that focus their oppression. The next step is to read together passages of Scripture, to see what they have to say about their situation. Then, after meditating on the Scripture that has been read together, they ask, "What are we going to do about our situation?" For them, the study of the Bible is not complete until it leads to some kind of action—a "praxis" or application of the text to their daily living.

Similarly, recent feminist interpretations have challenged both the content of Scripture and other methods of interpretation. "A feminist reading of the Bible requires both a transformation of our patriarchal understandings of God, Scripture, and the Church and a transformation in the self-understanding of historico-critical scholarship and the theological disciplines."[5] Based on this experience of oppression by a patriarchal tradition, feminist interpreters have made major contributions to our understanding of the role of women in the Bible. In addition, they have used the biblical view of liberation to criticize other passages within the Bible that promote the subordination of women. The purpose of their approach is to establish a dialogue between the Bible and the way in which women deal with contemporary social structures. Note, however, that there is one important point at which this feminist position adopts a functional view of biblical authority. When the Bible pictures a society dominated by males, feminists insist that such patterns must be rejected. Such patterns belong to particular cultures of the past; they simply do not reveal God's intention for the role of women. In other words, at this point in the dialogue, the Bible no longer has the stronger voice, certainly not the voice of God.

Let the Texts Speak for Themselves

A third general approach, in part a reaction to the "dangers" of historical criticism, is *to let the texts speak for themselves*. If you were to follow this approach, you would not really be concerned with the process by which the text received its present form; you would be interested only in the final product. You would not be concerned with the author's intention, since you would feel that we have no way to recover it. You would not be particularly interested in the historical situation of the author or his audience, since you would regard these as basically irrelevant to the meaning of the text. This approach is primarily interested in the biblical text as literature. There are several different methods or techniques used in this approach, but all of them are indebted in one way or another to contemporary literary criticism.

For example, "rhetorical criticism" focuses on the literary techniques that the biblical authors used to make their points. "Reader response" criticism focuses on the effect the text has on the reader, so that in some respects it is close to the "dialogue" mentioned above. Other contemporary authors are more concerned with understanding each biblical document in terms of its place within the overall collection of Scripture; thus this method is often called "canonical" criticism.

There are several advantages to this third approach. First, you can avoid asking historical questions that seem to have no conclusive answers. Second, you can focus on the primary sources, the biblical texts, and pay less attention to other ancient texts that contain similar ideas. This makes the texts much more accessible to you as a nonspecialist. Third, this approach allows the text to unfold a variety of new meanings. What Paul is saying to you in 1 Corinthians 13 is not limited by what he was trying to say to his original audience. For all of these reasons, it is not hard to see why these ways of looking at the text have met with an enthusiastic "reader response."

At the same time, if you cut the Bible loose from its original moorings, the great danger is that you may lose a sense of direction. Unless we know something about the original situation, then it is hard for us to say that one interpretation makes sense, while another one is just plain wrong. For that reason, I will continue to use information gained from reconstructing the past, but I will also draw on these more recent methods where they are useful.

HOW TO USE THE BIBLE
IN CHRISTIAN ETHICS

When I wrote *Black Power and Christian Responsibility* more than twenty years ago, there was almost no discussion of how to relate the Bible and Christian ethics. Fortunately, several good books on this topic have appeared since then, especially in the past few years, and they are included in the bibliography. In turn, most of them will refer you to other sources.

We have looked at different claims you might make for the authority of the Bible and at different ways of reading it, so you will not be surprised to find the same kind of variety when we ask how to use the Bible in Christian ethics. Obviously, the rest of this book explores this question. In this introductory section, we will only take a brief look at two of the most common ways of using Scripture. Several other approaches are mentioned in the books included in the bibliography for this chapter. I call these two approaches "ways that won't work." I do not mean that they are worthless, or that they have no place in Christian moral reflection. I simply mean that they are not adequate, for reasons I will explain later.

The Bible as Moral Recipes

Probably the most common approach is to treat the Bible as a set of *moral recipes*. It suggests that, if you have a problem, all you have to do is turn to the Bible, find the right passage, and find what it tells you to do. Are you anxious? Then read Psalm 23. Are you feeling guilty? Then read Psalm 51. Are you considering a divorce and want to know what to do? Then find all the passages in which divorce is mentioned. These examples treat the Bible as a collection of commandments, rules, and advice that can speak to every possible contingency in the modern world. Indeed, the Bible clearly contains material of this kind, both laws and wise sayings; that is not the issue. Rather, the issue is whether the Bible alone can solve all of our problems, or whether we need to refer to other sources of moral insight such as the traditional teachings of the church, the ideas of famous moral philosophers, and the discoveries of modern social and natural sciences.

One danger in this way of relating the Bible and ethics is that it reduces the moral life to a Christian *legalism*. If you want to be a Christian, it suggests, all you need to do is to find the correct rule and live by it. On the other hand, it implies that if you do obey, then God owes you a reward. As Paul observed so clearly about the kind of legalism he was criticizing, it leads inevitably to pride, to a "holier than thou" attitude. A film called *The Holy Ghost People* documents a worship service in a congregation of "holy rollers" in rural West Virginia. Members of the congregation believe in speaking in tongues and faith healing as signs of the presence of the Holy Ghost; they also handle poisonous snakes and drink poison when the Spirit moves them. At one point in the service, when the leader is telling them to pray for God's healing, he says, "If God isn't making you well, it's because you don't believe. If you have faith, God is obligated to heal you." This makes Christian morality a kind of contractual obligation. It badly oversimplifies biblical morality.

Another problem with this way of dealing with the Bible is that it is *selective*. The tendency is to look for those texts that tell you what you wanted to know, a procedure we generally term "proof texting." The temptation is to ignore or reject those passages you find offensive. If you favor prohibition, you are likely to ignore the advice to Timothy to "use a little wine" (1 Timothy 5:23); on the other hand, the passage clearly refers to medicinal uses and cannot be used to support substance abuse. A more humorous example is the story of the man who wanted biblical advice on how to face a serious personal problem. Letting his Bible drop open, he pointed to the text that read "And Judas went and hanged himself." Not satisfied with that advice, he repeated the steps, opened to another page, and let his finger fall on the text "Go and do likewise." In this particular instance, he had the good sense not to follow the command.

A third problem with treating the Bible as a collection of moral recipes is the tendency to take advice *out of context*. That was illustrated in the example I just gave. I heard a glaring example of this error while driving through South Carolina at the end of December in 1989. A radio preacher was condemning the summit meeting between presidents Bush and Gorbachev in the Mediterranean because the book of Revelation was written in the Mediterranean. Gorbachev, of course, was the "beast" whose number was 666. Also, Revelation used "Babylon" as a code for Rome, and since Gorbachev was controlled by the Pope in Rome and Bush had just visited the Pope, this preacher obviously felt that the antichrist was present in full force at that meeting! All of that, of course, takes the message of Revelation completely out of context; John had no knowledge of the Pope or of Russia or of the United States, so it is a mistake to try to suggest that he was predicting modern world politics.

Finally, another weakness faces us if we look to the Bible to find simple recipes. Many of the most complex modern problems are ones on which *the Bible is silent*. It says nothing about nuclear weapons or biological warfare, about AIDS or organ transplants, about world hunger or the depletion of the world's natural resources. This silence of the Bible is one reason why the recipe approach tends to limit Christian morality to questions of personal behavior, since the Bible has so little to say about larger social issues.

The Bible as a Source of Theological and Moral Principles

Is there a way to avoid these pitfalls? One major alternative is to treat the Bible as a source of *theological and ethical principles*. Instead of focusing on particular texts, this approach tries to draw out from the Bible some great themes that can guide the moral life.

One example of such a theme would be "love." Paul certainly ranked it as the greatest of the Christian virtues. Following him, Augustine reflected on the way in which our self-love distorts our love for God. Our passion for God drives us, but we constantly focus that passion on worldly objects that cannot fully satisfy us. Augustine's famous line "My heart is restless until it finds its rest in Thee" sums up this insight. The most famous American writer on Christian social ethics of the last generation was Reinhold Niebuhr, who based much of his work on Paul and Augustine.[6] For him, love is a transcendent norm. That is, love ought to guide us in all of our relationships. Unfortunately, however, we fail to let it do that. On the one hand, our pride or self-love leads us to deny our need for God. On the other hand, we also tend to neglect God just because we are so preoccupied with day-to-day activities and pleasures. Even more critical, according to Niebuhr, is the fact that love is an impossible norm for large social groups. Therefore, love is an "impossible possibility"; the most we can hope for in social and political relationships is justice. Justice is not love, but it comes as close to love as we can expect. For this whole tradition, then, biblical ethics can be summarized in the principle of selfless love.

Another example of an ethical principle drawn from the Bible is found in the Social Gospel movement. During the early decades of the twentieth century, this movement was an important way of applying the biblical message to social and economic issues such as poverty and labor relations. Walter Rauschenbusch, a pastor in Hell's Kitchen in Manhattan's West Side and later a professor at Rochester Theological Seminary, found the heart of the gospel in Jesus' proclamation of the coming Kingdom of God.[7] For Rauschenbusch and others in the Social Gospel movement, the Kingdom of God was a realistic social program. If you really meant the prayer "Thy Kingdom come, on earth as it is in heaven," then you would be obligated to work for social justice. Other advocates of this kind of Christian "liberalism" summarized the gospel message as "the Fatherhood of God and the brotherhood of man." In fact, when Niebuhr later developed his "Christian realism," it was largely a reaction against what he saw as the naive optimism of the social gospel.

Martin Luther believed that Paul's phrase "justification by faith" summarized the Christian message. While this is not an ethical principle in the strictest sense, it is nevertheless a statement about the Christian's relationship to God that provides the motivation and direction for Christian morality. Similarly, as we noted earlier, the biblical idea of the "covenant" can also provide an important theological framework. In recent years, a number of scholars have talked about "peace-making" as an ethical principle derived from the Bible, especially from Jesus' message.

This way of relating the Bible and ethics has the advantage of looking at the Bible as a whole, rather than focusing on selected verses that are often taken out of context. Rather than pick and choose, it takes seriously the authority of the entire biblical message.

At the same time, there are some serious disadvantages to this approach, so that I have called it one of the ways that won't work. First, this way of using the Bible tends to be *nonhistorical*.

It reduces the Bible to very general and abstract principles of theology or ethics. It tends to ignore the concrete social settings in which Isaiah and Jesus and Paul delivered their messages. It overlooks the specific issues that prompted the sayings and/or writings. For example, Paul first mentions "justification by faith" in Galatians, when he is trying to convince the Christians there not to revert to the law as a basis for the moral life. He does not mention it, however, in writing to the Corinthians, who were abusing their Christian freedom in ways Paul considered immoral. Second, this approach also tends to be *selective*. Given the great variety of viewpoints within Scripture, if you pick one theme, you have to ignore others that are equally important. Amos emphasizes justice, while Hosea emphasizes faithfulness and covenant love. Love may be the most important requirement for Paul, but it is inseparable from faith and hope. First Peter and Revelation emphasize the importance of patient endurance in the face of suffering. No one theme, then, can fully express the biblical message.

There are several other ways in which people have tried to relate the Bible to Christian ethics, but these two represent the most important approaches. In the pages ahead, we will look first at the way in which biblical writers speak about the moral life, and then look at the way in which different churches have used the Bible in developing their moral positions. Out of that study, I hope to present a position that will work, that is, that will avoid some of the dangers and pitfalls we have seen.

Exercise 3

Now that you have read this chapter, answer the following questions and be prepared to discuss them.

1. *Which one of the arguments for biblical authority is closest to your own view? Why?*
2. *Which approach to reading the Bible appeals to you the most? Why?*

3. Is the Bible helpful to you in making moral choices or in deciding how you should live as a Christian? If not, why not? If so, how do you use it?

LITERACY GUIDE FOR THE NEW TESTAMENT

1. How many books are there in the New Testament?
2. How many Gospels are there? Name them.
3. Who wrote more books of the New Testament than anyone else?
4. Where can you find the Sermon on the Mount?
5. Which book gives us a history of the early church?
6. What is the name of the last book of the New Testament?

PART ONE

BIBLICAL STYLES
OF MORAL REFLECTION

2

Law as the Basis for the Moral Life

What do you think of first when you hear the term "law"? Do you think of specific rules, such as traffic laws or the Ten Commandments? Do you think about a more general type of behavior—for example, about what it means to be a "law-abiding citizen," or about what the New Testament means by love as a "law" or a "new commandment"? What does the term mean to you?

As Americans, most of us have a positive view of the role law plays in our civic life. We are unique in having worked out a written constitution at the very beginning of our life as "united" states, a fact that Seymour Lipset recognized by calling us "the first new nation."[1] For that reason, all of our public life is ultimately subject to the rule of law, and appeals to "law and order" are always popular in times when our civic life is disturbed by crime or violence. We are apt, then, to think of "law" in terms of a whole system of written codes, drafted by legislatures and tested by the courts.

This experience can be helpful as we approach the Bible. Our laws help to define our society. When we pass and enforce and interpret laws, we are actually spelling out our vision of society as we would like it to be. Similarly, when we look at the biblical understanding of law, what we really discover is a vision of society under the rule of God.

On the other hand, our experience may mislead us. For one thing, we tend to think of the law primarily in terms of the civil community, of a state that is basically secular. The Bible, in contrast, is primarily a blueprint for a religious community. It does not make a distinction between "religious" and "secular" obligations, since all life should be brought under God's rule, but the laws are clearly intended for people standing in a special, covenant relationship to God.

Our experience may also mislead us because we associate laws with an extensive criminal justice system. Our legal system assumes that we are adversaries. As a result, we find ourselves becoming an increasingly litigious society, in which minor disagreements become court cases. Just think of the number of TV programs that dramatize law enforcement or even court cases. The Bible, in contrast, says very little about the administration of justice. In fact, Paul warns the Corinthians to resolve their disputes within the community rather than taking them to court. We must understand the biblical writers on their own terms and not read our own ideas into the ancient texts.

THE TORAH (LAW) IN ISRAEL

Exercise 4

Before you continue reading this chapter, take a look at some Old Testament passages: Exodus 19–23, 34–35; Leviticus 19–26; and Deuteronomy 5–12, 26–27. As you read, ask yourself:

1. *What kind of literature is this?*
2. *What kinds of behavior are commanded or forbidden? Notice the kinds of issues that recur. See if you can group them into five or six categories.*
3. *What arguments or reasons are used to convince people to obey these laws?*

The Context of the Torah

The Torah has a specific *literary context*. The word "Torah" in Hebrew can mean "teaching" in a broad sense; it refers to the revelation of God's purpose for human life. Torah is also used in a narrower sense to refer to one section within the biblical literature; it locates God's revelation in the opening five books of the Bible. These books were the first ones in the Bible to receive their present form, so they represent the oldest part of the canon. The term "Torah" was later translated into Greek as "nomos" and into English as "law."

If we were to look at all five of these books (also known as the Pentateuch or five scrolls), we would discover several types of material—for example, the stories of the Patriarchs and the Exodus from Egypt and the wandering in the wilderness. Instead, our focus will be on the passages that you read in exercise 4. This is clearly legal material. We find the terms "laws" and "statutes" and "ordinances" repeated over and over. This type of ethical reflection has to do with obedience to God's commands. That much is obvious. What we must do is to understand how this kind of reflection occurs. We can begin by making two observations about the literature.

First, these laws are phrased in different ways. We are most familiar with the form found in the Decalogue or Ten Commandments: "Honor," "Remember," "You shall not." These are *absolute*. We are supposed to follow them without any qualifications or exceptions. On the other hand, if we look at Exodus 21:12–27, we find examples of *case* law. Each situation is conditional; it is introduced by "when" or "if" or "whoever" and recommends an appropriate punishment. These are early examples of "Let the punishment fit the crime." Both types of law are found in other literature of the Ancient Near East, but the absolute form plays an important part in the Torah.

Second, even a casual reading shows us different styles. The most logical conclusion is that originally there were several different collections or codes, which eventually were brought together in the Torah as we have it now. The final

version of the Pentateuch suggests that all the commandments were given by God directly to Moses at Mount Sinai,
but that is an idealized picture from a later time. In addition
to these differences of style, we can easily pick out laws
whose content applies only to situations much later in Israel's
history. In fact, the book of Deuteronomy tries to solve that
problem of chronology by presenting its material in the form
of Moses' farewell speech to the people of Israel; Moses an-
ticipates the problems they will face once they have settled in
the Promised Land.

In the earliest stage, these collections almost certainly passed
from one generation to the next by word of mouth, by oral
tradition. The transition to a written text was an important one,
because it gave the text a fixed character, similar to our own
written Constitution. The Ten Commandments were probably
one of the oldest parts of the collection; certainly they now
stand as the core of the Sinai event in Exodus 20. Note that
there is a slightly different version in Deuteronomy 5. Note also
that Exodus 34 also contains ten commandments, but these apply almost exclusively to ritual actions and so they are often
called the "Ritual Decalogue." Without taking time to analyze
them, we can simply point to other probable collections: Exodus 20:22–23:19, referred to as "the Book of the Covenant"
because of its close link to Exodus 19 and to the giving of the
Ten Commandments; Deuteronomy 12–26, the "Deuteronomic
Code" (whose discovery is described in 2 Kings 22–23); Leviticus 19–26, called the "Holiness Code" because of its repeated
command "You shall be holy" because "I am the Lord." Much
of the other material scattered throughout the Torah comes
from a later group of Priestly writers, who apparently gave the
final shape to these five books. There may be elements of
a "Priestly Code" in Leviticus 1–7, 11–16, and in Numbers
28–29. If you are interested in learning more about these literary questions, you may consult any standard introduction to
the Old Testament or one of the other books listed in the bibliography for this chapter.

Social Context

We must remember that the Torah also has a *social context*. This process of collecting did not occur in a vacuum. The laws reflect a vision of society, as we noted above. The priests were primarily responsible for putting Israel's laws into writing, so we should not be surprised that the Torah reflects their vision of a religious community. That fact explains why Deuteronomy emphasizes the importance of getting rid of local sanctuaries, so all the people may worship in the one sanctuary that God has provided. (The reference, of course, is to the first Temple in Jerusalem before its destruction in 587 B.C.E.) That also explains why so many of the laws are concerned with the proper way to offer sacrifices, since that was the priests' responsibility. The Hebrew Bible gives glimpses of several ways in which the laws were interpreted at different periods of Israel's history. David apparently took over what we would call judicial functions, and his son Solomon is pictured as the wise man able to resolve the conflict between two mothers claiming the same child. At other points, we find references to "the Elders" who sat at the city gates to hear and decide disputes. When the monarchy collapsed and Israel's leaders were carried off into exile, the power to interpret the laws apparently passed to the priests. They codified the Torah. They created the vision of a new Temple, which is described most clearly in Ezekiel 40–48. They supervised the rebuilding of the Temple in the years 520–515 B.C.E., as we know from reading Ezra and Nehemiah. As long as that Second Temple survived, the priests remained the authoritative interpreters of the written Torah. During the time of Jesus, they were known as the Sadducees. There were other voices emerging, of course, but they are not really heard until later. Those who control the texts control the vision.

The Content of the Torah

The second question in exercise 4 concerned the kinds of behavior that were commanded or prohibited. These laws give us a picture of the social structure that existed at the time, and also a picture of the way in which obedience to God should be reflected in all of life. Take a look at your list. What issues did you find? What follows is my classification; compare it to your own.

The largest number of the laws apply to *worship*. They prescribe the proper way to make offerings and sacrifices. They describe the building of the Ark of the Covenant and the Tabernacle. They warn against witchcraft and sorcerers and human sacrifice. Most of these reflect the concerns of the priests.

Another group of laws apply to *social relations*. They cover family relationships. They tell how to deal with neighbors and with strangers.

A third group deal with *economic* behavior. They warn against cheating and taking bribes. They warn against cutting the crops so thoroughly that nothing is left in the field for the poor. All of these rules presuppose an agricultural setting.

A major concern is with *purity*, making a distinction between what is clean and what defiles. Some of this occurs in a ritual context (for example, Leviticus 6–7). However, these injunctions also apply to social relations, such as avoiding contact with a corpse or with a woman during menstruation (see Leviticus 21–22). This category overlaps with the first two, but it is worth mentioning separately because it has so much to do with the motivation for moral behavior.

Finally, we need to notice the special attention given in these laws to the *underprivileged*: the poor, the sojourners (resident aliens), and strangers. Even though these people may not belong to the covenant community, they are singled out for special treatment.

In these laws, then, we have a blueprint for the kind of human community God intends. Later rabbis counted 613 separate commandments. If everyone would only observe these commandments, Israel would be a holy community, an ideal society. Now, ask yourself two questions. First, if you and I were to sit down and design a modern utopia, don't you think we could do a better job? So many issues that are important today, such as drug use, are not even mentioned. Many other commandments are basically blue laws; if they were not part of Scripture, we would probably take them off the books. Second, do you think it is possible to follow these commandments literally? For example, those laws designed for farmers are simply impossible to follow in an urban setting. Other laws presuppose the Temple and its sacrificial system, which has not existed since the Romans destroyed it in 70 C.E. If we cannot obey these laws as written, then we have to find some way to interpret them. We will have to return to that issue at the end of this chapter.

Arguments for Obedience to the Law

What arguments or reasons for obeying these laws did you find in your reading? We are exploring the Torah as one style of moral reasoning. Therefore, we must not only pay attention to the kinds of behavior that are acceptable, as we have just done; we must also ask *why* people should behave in that way.

At one level, we could argue that the punishments themselves are a pragmatic reason for reinforcing desirable behavior. If you break the law, be prepared to suffer the consequences. That is probably an unspoken rationale, but we do not often find it used as an argument. Occasionally other pragmatic reasons are given for certain actions. The Israelites are to be kind to strangers, remembering that they were once strangers in the land of Egypt. They should not give bribes, since "a bribe blinds the officials" to what is just. These explanations are also rare.

One of the main rationales for moral behavior is *historical*. The writers appeal to their memory of *what God has done for them*. This is not an abstract moral principle. It does not apply to all people in every situation. Rather, it appeals to their experience of God's revelation:

> You have seen what I did to the Egyptians, and how I bore you on eagles' wings and brought you to myself. Now, therefore, if you obey my voice and keep my covenant, you shall be my treasured possession out of all the peoples. Indeed, the whole

earth is mine, but you shall be for me a priestly kingdom and a holy nation. (Exodus 19:4–6)

Similar expressions are found throughout Deuteronomy (literally "the second law"). This experience created a dilemma for Israel, as it does for everyone who accepts these covenant obligations. If we are convinced that we are on God's side, then God must be on our side in the struggle against secular culture and against other religions. This conviction is apt to give us a sense of exclusiveness; it leads to a "holier than thou" attitude. The antidote is to remember that, as people of the covenant, we must witness to what God is doing in today's world in order to bring the world to acknowledge God's powerful love.

The other major appeal is *theological*. Israel's obedience is based on her knowledge of *what God is like*. Remember the phrase repeated in Leviticus at the end of many of the commandments: "I am the Lord." This appeal is not to an abstract essence but to those particular qualities that Israel had experienced. God *loves* them (see Deuteronomy 10:14–15); they are God's covenant people. Furthermore, God is *just*. The demand for justice in the community, then, is rooted in the character of God (see Deuteronomy 10:17–18). Finally, God is *holy*. In Leviticus, God's holiness is reason why we should strive for both ritual and moral perfection (see Leviticus 11:44–45). This is perhaps the most difficult aspect for us to understand; certainly it is the most difficult for us to achieve.

The Authority of the Torah

Let us summarize quickly this first pattern of thinking about the moral life. The authority of the Torah lies in its claim to reveal God's purpose for human life. That revelation consists of a set of rules and commandments, and these are embodied in a written document (the Torah). This Torah is therefore the "constitution" or basis for the life of God's people. It is a plan for the covenant community, not for a world government, although the hope is that other people will be attracted by their life-style and will want to accept Israel's God. The moral life consists of obeying these laws.

In practice, the authority of the Torah is that of a legal tradition. Late in Israel's history, when these laws were receiving their fixed form, the priests emerged as the custodians of the Torah. Their authority stemmed, at least in part, from their role as interpreters of the Torah. In the next part of this chapter, we will see if we can find the same pattern of moral reflection in the emerging Christian community.

WAS CHRIST THE END OF THE LAW?

Exercise 5

What do you think the New Testament says about "law"? Are Christians still obligated to live by rules such as the Ten Commandments? Or have we been freed from all such obligations, so that we now live only by the gospel? Jot down some of your first impressions. Then read some passages in Acts that describe how the early church dealt with this issue: 2:43–47; 6:1–7; 10:1–11:26; 15:1–35. You may also want to compare the account in Acts 15 with Galatians 2:1–10 and ask yourself if they are describing the same event. Are the participants the same? Is the main issue the same? Is the outcome the same?

The Historical Context

While Jesus and Paul were living, the focus of Jewish worship was the Temple in Jerusalem. The Torah remained the foundation document for Judaism, but by now several different schools of interpretation had emerged. The group with the most direct ties to the priestly tradition we have already discussed were the Sadducees, who insisted that the written Torah alone was a sufficient basis for Jewish life and practice. Growing in influence was a movement of lay teachers known as the Pharisees. They argued that at Mount Sinai God had given an oral as well as a written Torah. As inheritors of that oral tradition, the Pharisees were able to adapt the written Torah to new situations. Eventually, after the destruction of the Temple by the Romans, their position became the dominant one. Later, the teachings of these rabbis were collected in the Talmud and provide the foundation for modern Judaism. Another alternative was the monastic sect at Qumran, which rejected the leadership in Jerusalem and found in the Torah the basis for a life of greater moral purity.

The early Christians were part of this broader ferment within Judaism. They accepted the same Bible as their book. Jesus and Paul did not see themselves as beginning a new religion but as offering a new interpretation of the Jewish tradition. Indeed, Jesus' own message is close to that of the Pharisees, even though he does not appeal to their oral tradition, and Paul himself was actually a Pharisee before becoming a Christian.

After Jesus' death and resurrection, according to information in Acts and in Paul's letters, the Christian attitude toward the Torah went through three stages. The earliest group of Jewish-Christians (called "Hebrews" in Acts) continued to worship at the Temple and to insist on full obedience to the Torah as a condition for being a Christian. Acts 15 identifies some of them as believers who were still Pharisees. The "Hellenists" mentioned in Acts 6–7 were apparently more assimilated into the Greek culture of the time and held a more negative attitude toward the Temple. Soon, however, there emerged a third group which insisted that Gentiles (non-Jews) would be welcomed into the Christian community simply on a profession of faith in Jesus Christ; they would be exempt from the requirements of the Torah, including male circumcision and observance of the kosher food laws. Acts 10–11 marks the first step in this direction and identifies it with Peter. Jew and Gentile were able to eat together, breaking down the laws of purity. According to Acts 15, a summit meeting of early Christian leaders was held in Jerusalem to decide the basis on which Gentiles would be admitted into Christian fellowship. In Acts, the issue resulted in a compromise solution, imposing four general requirements but not the whole Torah. Paul's version of the same event in Galatians 2 insists that no conditions were imposed on the Gentiles, and that the Gentile mission was delegated to Paul. He is certainly the representative of that third point of view who is best known to us, although there must have been many others active in that mission. When the Temple and the city of Jerusalem were destroyed in the Jewish War of 66–70 C.E., that Gentile mission enabled Christianity to survive. As a result, Christianity was finally seen as a new religion and not as a continuation of Judaism.

Paul's Rejection of the Torah

In Romans 10:4, Paul insists that Christ is "the end of the Law." Because he was so convinced that Christ's death and resurrection had accomplished what the Torah was intended to do (namely, to declare humans righteous before God), he drew the conclusion that the Torah had failed and was no longer needed. Even though there are hints in Acts and in his own letters that Paul may have continued to observe the Torah, he risked his life to insist that the Torah was not binding on those Gentiles who became Christians. This was Paul's practice in the churches he founded. It was the message he conveyed in his letters, which form the earliest part of our New Testament. His view has helped to shape Christian thinking about the Law, particularly in Protestant circles.

Exercise 6

Read Galatians, especially 2:11–21 and 3:19–29; also Romans 1:16–3:31 and 7:1–25. Summarize in your own words what Paul says about the Law. What role should it play in a Christian's moral life?

Like other Jewish teachers of his time, Paul assumed that the Torah was a gift from God to show people how to achieve a right relationship to God (that is, "righteousness").[2] That was especially true of the Jews, who had the written Torah (Romans 2:17–3:20). It was also true for Gentiles, who had their conscience and "a law of nature" to tell them what was acceptable behavior (Romans 1:18–2:16, especially 2:14–16). However, Paul took a much more perfectionist view of the Law than his contemporaries. Unless people kept the whole Law, he argued, it could not deliver what it promised; it could not make people righteous. What this really boils down to, he insists in Romans 7:21–25, is a failure of our human will. We simply fail to do what we know we should do.

What, then, does the Law do? What are its functions? For one thing, it brings us knowledge of our sin, of our failure to measure up to what God expects of us (Romans 3:20). Even more serious is the fact that it provokes us to sin; it tempts us to do what is forbidden (Romans 7:7). A colleague of mine puts this in simple terms by saying, "Never tell a child not to put beans up his nose." The temptation is just too great. A third function that Paul mentions in Galatians 3:23–26 is that of a custodian. The Law was a kind of nursemaid or tutor, helping people to know God's will in the period before faith in Christ became a possibility.

We should realize at least two things about Paul's view. First, his rejection of the Torah is a conclusion and not a point of departure. Paul did not start by believing that the Torah had failed and then go looking for something better to take its place. Rather, he started with Christ's death and resurrection, which completed everything the Torah was meant to do and made it superfluous. Second, Paul did not base his claims on Jesus' own teachings about the Torah. Rather, Paul asserted that Christ's death and resurrection marked the beginning of a new creation and a new relationship to God.

Paul, then, rejected the idea of a community based on Law, on commandments and rules. For him, the whole pattern of moral reflection based on the Torah is doomed to failure. He has a much more dynamic view of the way in which the Christian community develops an ethos, which we will examine in chapter 6.

The Eclipse of the Torah

In addition to Paul's vigorous challenge to the Torah as the basis of the Christian life, we can find evidence that others in the early church took a similar position.

An impressive amount of evidence suggests that Mark was the first Christian to compose a "Gospel." This was essentially a new literary form. The content of the good news, as he says in 1:1, is that Jesus is "the Christ, the Son of God." Mark was also apparently writing for an audience of Gentile Christians, since he took time to explain several Jewish words and practices. In his summary of Jesus' ministry and message, Mark shows us a teacher who emphasized the moral aspects of the Torah and either ignored or criticized the ritual aspects.

Exercise 7

Read Mark 2:1–3:6, which reports a series of conflicts between Jesus and other Jewish leaders. As you read this brief section, ask yourself these questions about each incident. Who are the opponents? What is the issue? What is the outcome?

Mark 2:1–3:6 apparently existed as a very early collection of stories about Jesus' conflict with Jewish opponents over the proper way to interpret the Torah, which Mark incorporated into his Gospel. You will quickly note that in every case Jesus either violates some commandment in the Torah or opposes the way in which it was understood by his contemporaries. For example, he claims God's authority to forgive sins; he associates with those "sinners" who fail to observe the laws of purity; he refuses to fast; and he both feeds and heals on the Sabbath. You will also note that the conflict heightens so quickly that a plot to kill Jesus is hatched, even though in Mark's Gospel the sequel does not come until the beginning of chapter 14. Elsewhere, Mark reports a series of other typical cases in which Jesus offers a new interpretation of the Torah, and in which Jesus relaxes or sets aside the ritual requirements.

Among Jesus' followers, as we have already noted, it was only the earliest group that insisted on full obedience to the Torah. Within a generation, that group had essentially disappeared, and none of their writings (if they had any) have survived. The letter of James claims to speak for the earliest Jewish Christians, but as we shall see it does not insist on obedience to the whole Torah.

Very quickly the early church developed its own way of interpreting Scripture. Although the Hebrew Bible remained a source of authority for the early Christians, they no longer tried to observe it in a literal way. Different methods of interpretation can be seen emerging in Paul's letters, in Matthew's formula "so that the Scripture might be fulfilled," in Luke, in Hebrews, and elsewhere.

For all of these reasons, we can say that obedience to the Torah is not the primary mode of moral reflection in the New Testament. Why not? Primarily because of the decision to admit Gentiles into the Christian community without requiring them to convert to Judaism first. The church kept the Hebrew Bible but understood it in new ways, not simply as a moral code. The Torah was treated with respect but was not binding in all respects.

THE LAW IN EARLY CHRISTIANITY

Is there another way to answer the question about Christ as the end of the Law? Can we find, anywhere in the New Testament, a style of moral reasoning based on commandments and rules? There is evidence that a Christian legal tradition began to develop within the early church. When this happened, the basis for the moral life was not the Torah itself but rather a body of Christian instruction. In contrast to Paul, Matthew's Gospel does approach the moral life primarily in terms of obedience to the Law.

Exercise 8

1. Read the Sermon on the Mount, Matthew 5–7. Pay special attention to 5:17–20. These verses are found only in this Gos-

pel, so they give us a clue to the way in which Matthew understood Jesus' message.

2. Also, look closely at 5:21–48, a series of six contrasts or "an-
titheses" in which Jesus cites a passage from the Torah and
then gives his own interpretation of it.

3. Finally, look at Jesus' other sayings about the Law that Matthew records in 19:16–22 and 22:34–40.

The most obvious thing to say about Matthew's Gospel is that
he emphasizes *Jesus' authority* as a teacher and interpreter of
the Torah (for example, 7:28–29, at the conclusion of the Sermon on the Mount). In the set of contrasts in which he sets his
view of the Law over against other opinions, Jesus tells his followers how to understand and obey the claims of the Torah. In
contrast to the Sadducees, Jesus does not appeal only to the
written word, and in contrast to the Pharisees, he does not appeal to an oral tradition. Instead, he teaches on his own authority by saying "but I say to you." The debates between Jesus and
the Pharisees actually reflect the situation more than a generation later, at the time when Matthew wrote his Gospel. Following the destruction of Jerusalem, as we noted, Christianity
finally emerged as a new religion, and it had to compete with
the rabbis (successors of the Pharisees) over the right way to
interpret Scripture. Matthew presents Jesus as the true interpreter, the one who truly knows and reveals God's will. Therefore, Christians must not only study the commandments but
also keep them and teach them (5:19). To keep the Law now
means to keep Jesus' words (7:24–28).

There is no question that Matthew's Gospel is the blueprint
for a new religious community, based on the life and especially
on the teachings of Jesus. If we ask about the *content* of the
moral life, what we find is not so much a new set of rules as a
series of examples. The Beatitudes describe a life-style marked
by humility and meekness. If you follow this way of life, you
may be persecuted in this world, but you will receive God's
blessing in the world to come ("the kingdom of heaven"). The

difficult passage in 5:17–20 links the keeping of the Law to the coming of the Kingdom; the Law remains in effect until "all is accomplished." Also, the "righteousness" of Jesus' disciples should exceed that of the Jewish teachers. Matthew then records six examples of this in the contrasts that you read. In each case, Jesus quotes a verse from the Torah, or at least a way in which people might have understood it. Then he offers a new and often radical understanding of it. Jesus' point is that righteousness means more than simply avoiding certain actions; you must avoid the attitudes and behavior that leads to those actions. In 6:33 Matthew records a saying of Jesus' that pulls together these two emphases. Christians are to seek first God's Kingdom and God's righteousness.

In addition to these themes, we find illustrations of another kind of life-style that the gospel demands: faith. Surprisingly, the best examples of faith are those outside Jesus' inner circle: a centurion (8:5–13), the anonymous people who bring a paralyzed friend to be healed (9:2), a woman suffering from a hemorrhage (9:20–22). By contrast, his own disciples are often portrayed as having little faith (6:30; 8:23–27 and 14:22–36, both sea scenes; and 17:14–21).

A third set of examples has to do with unselfish love. Even though Matthew and Paul disagree in their understanding of righteousness, they both agree that when your life is motivated by love for both your neighbors and your enemies, you have fulfilled the Law (5:44; 19:19; 22:39). The parable of the last judgment, found only in Matthew's Gospel, illustrates this kind of love for those in need (25:31–46).

Elsewhere in this Gospel, through Jesus' stories and parables and his own dramatic acts, Matthew tells us, as his readers, how we are supposed to live as Jesus' followers. In the strict sense, these are not rules or commandments but examples of how to pursue a life of perfection.

Matthew, then, gives us a clear picture of the moral life that ought to mark the community of faith. Now we need to go one more step and ask what kind of *arguments* Matthew uses. Why should we live that way? Once again, Matthew's answer may surprise us. Some of the emphases in this Gospel are not found anywhere else, or at least not to the same extent. We have to realize that Matthew was applying Jesus' teaching to problems confronting the churches for which he was writing, especially the final split with the Jewish synagogues. In that context, we can understand the rationale for Christian morality. Christians are to strive to be "perfect," as God is perfect (5:48; 19:21). That perfection is basically the same as the righteousness we have already discussed. It is also the same as "doing God's will" (7:21).

On the other hand, Matthew's Gospel emphasizes God's future (eschatological) reward and punishment more than any other New Testament writing except the book of Revelation. The Beatitudes promise the blessings of God's Kingdom on those who live a Christian life-style now. In this world, and even within the church, we cannot be sure who is eligible for such a reward. Only the last judgment will reveal that (for example, 12:36 and 25:46). Both the good grain and the weeds exist together until "the close of the age" (13:24–30, 37–43). The dramatic imagery of God's final judgment does serve, in Matthew's Gospel, as a warrant or argument for the moral life.

The other New Testament book that seems to place the greatest emphasis on the place of the Law is James. Elsewhere in the New Testament, James is identified as "the brother of the Lord" and as the leader of the early Jewish-Christian community in Jerusalem. You probably remember him from your reading of Acts 15, where he proposed the compromise solution. Nothing in the epistle, however, identifies the author, except that he assumes the *authority of a teacher*; and the early conflict over the admission of Gentiles to the church is not even mentioned here. Whoever the author, and whenever the epistle was written, it is a marvelous picture of a sectarian community. It is not oriented toward the world but rather toward preserving its own identity and purity. There is no evidence of missionary activity, but there is a strong emphasis on brotherly love, on care for widows and orphans, on visiting the sick, on regular prayer, and on self-discipline.

Exercise 9

Read James 1–2 (and, if you have time, the other three chapters).

1. What does the author say about the Law in 1:25 and 2:8–12? What "law" does he mean? What authority should it have for his Christian readers?
2. Is his view closer to that of Paul or Matthew? If you had to write to one of the three for advice, which one would you choose? Why?

James is concerned with very practical problems, which we will examine more closely in chapter 5. If we were members of the community to which James was writing, we would have to learn how to nurture our own self-control, so that we could demonstrate the true religion of brotherly love. Is this religion based on obedience to the Law? On the one hand, he does speak about a "perfect law" in 1:25 and a "royal law" in 2:8. Apparently, then, he views this as one of the "perfect gifts" from God mentioned in 1:17. At first reading, it looks as though the author means the Torah, particularly since in 2:10 he echoes Paul's idea about the need to keep the whole Law. This is followed in the next verse by a direct quotation from the Ten Commandments, to illustrate the need to keep *all* of the laws.

On the other hand, "Law" seems to have a very different meaning than it did in the Old Testament. James does not refer at all to the ceremonial aspects of the Torah; this epistle is concerned with our moral life as Christians, not with our ritual behavior. The law he describes is a very flexible one. As he says twice, it is a "law of liberty" (1:25; 2:12). James does not even use the word "commandment," and when he refers to specific verses from the Torah (2:8, 11; 4:2) it is to illustrate a point, not to impose a requirement. When he argues that faith without works is dead (2:14–26), he does not attack Paul directly, but he does attack a way of misreading Paul that ignores the importance of the moral life. The "royal law" is the law of love for our neighbor. It is this law, and not the whole of the Torah, which should guide the moral actions and moral reflection of the Christian community.

The core of this new legal tradition is Jesus' summary of the Law. Over and over, New Testament writers cite Leviticus 19:18 ("You shall love your neighbor as yourself") as the fulfillment of the Torah, even when they do not explicitly connect this summary with Jesus himself. It is striking that most writers quote only the love commandment, only the second half of Jesus' summary of the Law. Paul does this in Galatians 5:14 and again in Romans 13:8–10. James does it in 2:8.

The longest discussion of the love commandment is found in 1 and 2 John. To love God, and to love Jesus as a child of God, is to keep the commandments (1 John 5:1–3). Love for the neighbor is the "new commandment" (1 John 2:7–8; 3:11). The author clearly has in mind the words of Jesus in John 14–15. However, he also suggests that the commandment is not completely new, meaning that it is consistent with the Torah. Unfortunately, "love one another" has a restricted meaning in these letters of John. Nothing is said here about loving one's enemies. Instead, there has been a split within the community, and those who have left are criticized for their failure to love and their failure to keep the commandments.

In these letters, the *content* of the love commandment remains quite general. There are no specific rules to follow. The basic *argument* is that God's love has been revealed in Jesus Christ and in the Christian fellowship. Finally, the *authority* of the author is made clear, especially in 2 and 3 John, where he identifies himself as "the elder."[3]

By the end of the first Christian century, the church began to focus on building a firm institutional base for the future. It did this in part by defining church offices more precisely (developing job requirements!) and by agreeing on a fixed body of teaching or doctrine that was acceptable. We can see that phase of the early church's life clear in the pastoral letters (1 and 2 Timothy and Titus). It comes as no surprise, then, that in 1 Timothy 1:8–11 "the law" does not seem to mean the Torah at all.

Instead, it is connected to "sound doctrine" promoted by qualified teachers. The function of the law is to convict and restrain vices. The development of a Christian legal tradition is well under way.

SUMMARY

Early Christianity, then, did begin to develop a legal tradition of its own, but it was not tied to a written code. It did not ignore the Jewish Torah, but it filtered that Torah through the ministry and teachings of Jesus. Paul actually speaks of loving one's neighbor as fulfilling "the law of Christ." Matthew closes the Sermon on the Mount with Jesus' saying that we are wise if we hear his words and do them. James calls it the "law of liberty."

The basic *context* is the need of the early church to develop a new style of moral reflection. The Christians were aware of themselves as a covenant community, but the Torah no longer defined them in the same way that it did Judaism. As the hope for Christ's immediate return began to fade, the church began to develop a body of moral instruction. The *content* of this moral tradition, as we have seen in Matthew and James and the letters of John, is fairly general. The focus is almost exclusively on what the members of the community must do to remain faithful. The *arguments* are basically an appeal to what God has done in Jesus Christ, to the presence of the new creation and to its coming fulfillment. Finally, as in the case of the Torah, *authority* passes to a body of interpreters. At first these were simply teachers, but in later New Testament documents the bishops and deacons and elders are the ones who define and enforce the moral tradition.

Exercise 10

We have looked at "law" as one pattern of moral reflection. We find it most clearly in the Torah, see it fading in Paul and Gentile Christianity, and then see it emerge as a new Christian legal tradition.

Law as the Basis for the Moral Life

1. Which of these three attitudes toward the Law do you find most appealing? Why?
2. Do you think it is all right to treat the Bible as a book of rules or a code of laws? Why or why not? Give some examples of individuals or groups that use the Bible in this way.

3

Prophecy as a Call to Moral Action

Who were the prophets, and why should we listen to them? There were, of course, prophets in other cultures, but the ones most familiar to us are those whose words have been preserved in the Old Testament. Were they men with long robes and shaggy heads of hair, pointing toward heaven and calling down God's judgment on a faithless people, as they are often pictured in religious art? Were they visionaries, trying to predict events that would take place years or centuries later? Were they powerful figures in their own times, or were they dangerous fanatics who were hated by both religious and political leaders?

Exercise 11

Before we look at their message, sharpen your own mental picture of these ancient figures. Jot down five or six characteristics you would use to describe them: temperament, life-style, themes, or whatever else you think is important. If you are in a group, share your impressions with others and see if you can come up with a composite description.

Then ask yourself if there is anyone in our own time who has those same characteristics. Would you be willing to call that person a "prophet"?

PROPHECY IN ISRAEL

We shall look at the context of prophecy in Israel before digging into an overview of the content, with special emphasis on the prophets' view of the social order and authority.

The Context of Israelite Prophecy

The *literary context* is fairly clear. In the Hebrew Bible, the section known as "the prophets" received its present form about two hundred years after the Torah, or about 200 B.C.E. That collection, however, included the books from Joshua through Kings, which we now treat as historical books. In the Christian canon, the longest prophetic books are those of Isaiah, Jeremiah, and Ezekiel. The writings of the other prophets—those at the end of the Old Testament—are treated as separate books. Historical information about the period of the prophets is found in 1 and 2 Kings and also in 1 and 2 Chronicles.

The process by which this literature received its present shape is a complex one that we will have to ignore, except for two notes. First, some prophetic "books" are collections of material from different times and places. That is especially true of Isaiah, which includes material covering a span of almost two hundred years. When interpreting these books, then, we need to know as much as we can about their historical setting. Second, and unfortunately, the original oracles or sayings were almost always delivered orally, and they were also passed on by word of mouth for some time before they were written down. For that reason, we often cannot tell the precise setting in which the words were first spoken, even though we can know the general context.

Because of the process by which the literature developed, the *social context* is also hard to reconstruct. The *origins* of Old Testament prophecy are obscure. Occasionally a prophet (*nabi'* in Hebrew) appears who speaks for God and acts as a military adviser, like Deborah in Judges 4:4–10. Other old texts refer to a "seer," but 1 Samuel 9:9 explains that this term was gradually replaced by the term "prophet." More often, the origins are associated with bands of ecstatic prophets who abandoned themselves to an emotional frenzy. When Elijah challenges the prophets of Baal to a bull roast (1 Kings 18:20–29), we are given a vivid picture of them hopping about the altar and cutting themselves with spears and lances. When Saul comes into contact with a band of such prophets, he gets so carried away that he strips himself and lies motionless all day and all night (1 Samuel 19:18–24).

The *development* of prophecy from these origins covers a period of roughly three hundred years. During much of this period, the Ancient Near East was involved in a series of conflicts. Israel itself was divided after the death of Solomon into the Northern Kingdom (Israel) and the Southern Kingdom (Judah). They fought periodically with each other, and with Syria, until the Northern Kingdom fell to the Assyrians in 721 B.C.E. The Southern Kingdom fell to the Babylonians in 587 B.C.E., and the leading citizens were carried off into exile. We can put things into some kind of perspective when we realize that the same kinds of conflicts have continued in recent years: between Israel and her neighbors, between Iran and Iraq, between various forces in Lebanon, and between Iraq and Kuwait. Most of the prophets were aware of these conflicts and spoke about them. The first great prophet, Elijah, was active in the Northern Kingdom during the ninth century B.C.E. He remains a prototype of the independent prophet, even though we do not have a record of his sayings. During the eighth century B.C.E., Amos and Hosea delivered their messages in the North, while Isaiah of Jerusalem (whose record is found in chapters 1–39 of that book) and Micah were active in the South. Jeremiah was active before and during the fall of Judah. So was Ezekiel, although the bulk of his work falls during the Exile, as do chapters 40–66 of Isaiah. These figures provide the genius of the prophetic movement; the others are minor. Their main concern was to speak to their contemporaries, so our first task is to understand them in their own times.

The *functions* of the prophets vary. Some apparently served as royal advisers, presumably as military consultants. Nathan served David in this way, although not always telling David what he wanted to hear. Many, like Isaiah of Jerusalem and Jeremiah, had access to the king even if they were not on the royal payroll. Others were apparently attached to one of the sanctuaries; Jeremiah identifies himself with the priests who were assigned to the Temple in Jerusalem but who lived outside the city in Anathoth (1:1). Still others remained independent of any "professional" context. Amos was one of these, and Amos insisted, "I am no prophet, nor a prophet's son; but I am a herdsman, and a dresser of sycamore trees" (7:14). Recently, scholars have argued that the leading prophets may have had "schools" or groups of disciples. In Jeremiah 36, for example, we learn that Baruch acted as a scribe for the prophet and copied down his words. Although other evidence is limited, such schools would help us to understand who actually collected and preserved the prophet's words.

The Content
of the Prophetic Message

In the last chapter, when we looked at the Torah, we asked what kinds of behavior were prohibited or criticized—in other words, what kinds of issues the Law addressed. Now we need to do the same thing for the prophets.

Exercise 12

Read as many of the following chapters as you can: Amos 4, 7–8; Hosea 1, 3–4, 11; Isaiah 1, 11, 40, 42, 55; Jeremiah 1, 7, 18, 23, 31, 36. Try to keep the historical setting in mind. If you are in a group, several of you can take one prophet and report back, or each person can take a different chapter. Ask yourself these questions as you read:

1. *What issues or problems were they addressing?*
2. *What advice did they give?*

3. *What arguments (appeals) did they use to back up their advice?*

Let me suggest that there were three major challenges or problems facing these prophets. There were many more specific issues, but most of them fell into one of these categories.

One major problem was the *religious competition* posed by the older, indigenous Canaanite worship of Baal. From the time the Israelites began to settle in the land of Canaan, they were tempted to assimilate their monotheistic religion to that of the local polytheism. At a theological level, this was a conflict between two ways of understanding reality. Baal was a god of nature and fertility, with a female consort and a host of other gods and goddesses. Israel, on the other hand, worshiped one God, who ruled over all creation but who was also active in Israel's history. At a more practical level, the conflict was whether Israelites should worship at the many local shrines or "high places" where sacrifices could be offered to Baal or only at the central sanctuaries: Bethel in the Northern Kingdom and Jerusalem in Judah. Most of the prophets attacked the worship of Baal because it represented a loss of religious purity.

A second challenge was the threat of *foreign domination*. The prophets directed their advice to the immediate situation. Sometimes they warned against any foreign alliances that would weaken Israel's independence. At other times they warned against building up national security at too great a cost to domestic policies. Sometimes they warned the king not to panic when the city was being attacked. The most painful message of all was that God might not protect them any more, since they had broken their part of the covenant. On the whole, these prophets spoke perceptively about political events. Their "realism" held in tension the "word of God" and practical politics.

A third set of issues concerned *economic exploitation*. Amos, a southerner, delivered at least one of his oracles at Bethel, the major shrine in the North. He attacked those who "trample the head of the poor into the dust of the earth" (2:7), particularly the rich women (the "cows of Bashan" who "oppress the poor, who crush the needy" so that they can enjoy their vacation homes and their drinks, 3:13–4:3). It is no wonder that Amaziah, a local priest, considered Amos an outside agitator and told him to go home (7:10–13). Similarly, Isaiah attacked the "elders and princes" who were confiscating the property of the poor peasants. The prophets did not offer a Marxist critique, identifying poverty as a structural problem in Israelite society, but they did identify economic inequality as one of the major issues of their day. They focused on the widows and the orphans and the underprivileged. This is one of the points where the Torah and the prophetic critique are nearly identical.

The prophets, then, are "first and foremost interpreters of history."[1] They do not predict future events in the sense of offering a scheme or blueprint for future generations. While writing this chapter, I saw a sign in front of a church that declared, "Dramatic Prophetic Events Are About to Happen," suggesting that the prophets were predicting events at the end of the twentieth century. On the contrary, the main concern of the Old Testament prophets is to point out the consequences of the moral choices facing Israel. If Israel repents, they say, God may not destroy the nation. If Israel does not turn from other gods, avoid foreign entanglements, and establish justice, then God will let the people suffer the consequences of their own behavior. This is why the prophetic message is a call to moral action.

The Prophetic Arguments
for the Social Order

The prophets convey a vision of a community ruled by God, but unlike the Torah they do not define it in terms of rules and regulations. Also, except for Ezekiel, they do not give as much attention as the priests to ritual and ceremonial issues. What kind of arguments or appeals did they use, then, to support their advice?

First, in some cases, they actually appeal to the Torah. What surprises us is not that they do but that so few of them do. Only in the Northern tradition do we find a direct appeal to the Torah. Amos 2:4 condemns the people of Judah (his own country) "because they have rejected the law of the Lord, and have not kept his statutes." Hosea tells the Israelites that they "have forgotten the law of your God" (4:6). He even cites the second part of the Ten Commandments, which deal with social relationships, to say that the people have broken all of these.

The second form of appeal made by the prophets was to God's covenant with Israel, but in very different ways. In Amos and Hosea, the covenant is *conditional* on Israel's obedience. As long as the people are faithful, God will protect them. Once they have broken their side of the agreement, God is no longer bound by it. Amos feels that the situation has gone too far, so that it may be impossible to avoid God's judgment. Hosea draws on his own marriage to argue, by analogy, that Israel is an unfaithful marriage partner, or even a whore. He describes God's *hesed* ("mercy" or "covenant love") for Israel, and he begs the people to return that love. On the other hand, in Judah we find a different view of the covenant, which is often called a "royal theology." As Isaiah of Jerusalem expresses it, the king is a visible sign of God's commitment to the people. This covenant is *unconditional*; God will not let the nation or Jerusalem or the monarchy be destroyed. That is why the fall of Jerusalem was so hard to accept when it did happen, and Israel's confidence shifted to some future king (Messiah) who would restore her independence. A third view is found in Jeremiah 31:31–34, where he speaks of a *new covenant* that God will make with Israel, writing it on their hearts instead of tablets of stone. This is the primary source for the early Christian claim that God had made a "new covenant" or "new testament" with them. We can see two interesting ways of developing that theme in 2 Corinthians 3:1–3 and Hebrews 8–10. Finally, in Isaiah 40–55, we find a new development. Out of the chaos and despair of the Exile, the author of these poems affirms God's love not just for Israel but for all nations. The fall of Jerusalem does not mean that Israel's God is powerless. Rather, that very God is the creator of the universe and the ruler of all nations. Through Israel and her suffering, God is establishing a *universal covenant*.

A third appeal for reforming the social order is found in God's demand for *justice* and *righteousness*. The most famous passage expressing these themes is Amos 5:21–24. It is also followed closely in the early message of Isaiah (1:11–17) and in his hopes for a new king whose rule will be just and right (9:2–7 and 11:1–9). This is one of the strongest appeals anywhere in the Bible for a society in which economic and social discrimination have been removed.

Prophetic Authority

The prophets claim to have *direct access* to the will of God. They have been commissioned by God. They serve as God's messengers, so that they can speak with the authority of the One who has sent them.

How do they receive their message? There are a variety of ways, but let us notice just a few of them. Many of the prophets mention their visions. For example, in Amos 7–8, he reports a vision of locusts, of a judgment by fire, of a plumb line, and of a basket of summer fruit, all symbols of God's impending judgment. On other occasions, a prophet may report an experience of standing in the Heavenly Council (in the presence of God and the divine messengers), of actually hearing God speak, and of being commissioned to carry that message to his contemporaries. We find a vivid example of that in Isaiah 6, the call of the prophet, and this is echoed in Isaiah 40, the opening poem of that great anonymous prophet during the Exile. Another form of revelation is in trances, which we find especially in Ezekiel.

It is this claim to authority that separates the prophets from the priests and other interpreters of the Torah. Even though the prophets can appeal to the Torah and the covenant, they are not tied to a written tradition. They are not interpreters of individual texts. Instead, their authority is that of charismatic individuals, of inspired messengers of God's Word.

The prophets use *forms of communication* that dramatize their authority to speak for God.[2] Variations on "Thus says the Lord" make clear the source of the prophet's words. One favorite device is a courtroom scene, in which the prophet tells the people that God has a bone to pick with them (a "controversy"). Then either the prophet (or God directly) presents the complaint and announces the verdict, thus acting as both prosecuting attorney and judge. Other dramatic forms are symbolic actions and symbolic names. For example, while Jerusalem was under siege, Jeremiah bought a field in his home town of Anathoth to show his confidence that God would allow the exiles to return and possess the land again. Both Hosea and Isaiah gave their children names that would demonstrate the message they had seen and heard.

The problem with this claim to authority, of course, is that there can be *false prophets*. We read of more than one confrontation between the biblical prophets and their rivals, often "professional" prophets employed by the king or the Temple. Jeremiah 28 records a vivid clash between Jeremiah and Hananiah. Jeremiah was wearing a wooden yoke to symbolize Israel's bondage to Babylon. Hananiah broke the yoke and said that within two years Israel would be released. Later, Jeremiah received a message from God to replace the original yoke with one of iron. Involved in this argument are three possible ways of finding out which one was the true prophet. One is to test their message by later historical events. In this case, Jeremiah's reading of the situation was clearly more accurate, but that test does not always work, even for the biblical prophets. A second issue has to do with the content of their messages. Any prophet who promises peace rather than doom and destruction cannot be trusted, but both Isaiah of Jerusalem and Second Isaiah provide exceptions to that rule. A third issue is whether or not the prophet has received a divine commission; Jeremiah claimed that Hananiah had not, so that he was not a true prophet. Of course, Hananiah could make the same accusation. In a detailed study of the arguments used to distinguish true from false prophets, James L. Crenshaw concludes that none of the criteria used in the Old Testament are conclusive.[3] "The prophet's authority was likely maintained and supported in groups, and reinforced by his conformity with social expectations. But it was made real insofar as his behavior was accepted by others."[4] Then why were the words of these particular prophets finally accepted into the collection of Scripture, and others excluded? Ultimately, it was because their message, like that of the Torah, was seen as a true vision of God's purpose for the people of Israel.

Exercise 13

Think back to the picture of a "prophet" that you created in exercise 1. Then ask yourself these questions:

1. *Has your picture changed as a result of looking at these Old Testament figures?*
2. *If you had been one of their contemporaries, would you have believed them? Why or why not?*
3. *How would you decide today if a person has a legitimate claim to speak for God?*

PROPHECY IN EARLY CHRISTIANITY

Were there New Testament prophets? Our instinctive reaction is to answer no to that question, because there certainly is no collection of prophetic writings like those we have just examined. Can you think of anyone in the New Testament who fits your picture of a prophet? Yet if you will read just a few selected passages, you may be surprised what an important place prophecy played in the beginnings of the Christian church.

Exercise 14

Read the following passages: Matthew 11:7–15; Mark 8:27–33; Acts 11:27–30; 13:1; 15:32; 21:7–14; 1 Corinthians 12:27–31; 14:1–5; Revelation 1:1–3; 22:6–21. As usual, you may want to assign these passages to different people in your group. Ask yourself two questions, if you can find enough information in the passage:

1. *Who is called a prophet?*
2. *What qualifies that person to be a prophet?*

Let us look at the people who are called "prophets." In the passage in Matthew, Jesus identifies John the Baptist as "more than a prophet," who brings to a close the period of "the law and the prophets." Jesus goes on to identify him as Elijah, adding the phrase "who is to come" or "the coming one," which was probably another key term in Jewish expectations of the time.[5] In Mark 8:27–30, Jesus conducts his equivalent of a Gallup poll in order to test public opinion about his identity. All three opinions reflect the close link between the two figures in the popular views of the time: Jesus is John the Baptist returned to life, or Elijah, or a prophet.[6] (Mark 6:14–16 reports that Herod chose the third of those options.) Indeed, the belief that Jesus was a prophet is found in virtually all strands of Gospel materials: for example, Matthew 21:11, 46; Luke 24:19; John 6:14.

The Acts of the Apostles, the companion volume to Luke's Gospel, is an idealized portrait of the early church. Yet the picture of a Spirit-filled community is consistent with what we find in other sources for the early stage of Christianity. In Acts, we find sixteen different people who are called prophets. Some of them appear to move from place to place, either as a regular pattern (11:27) or on a specific mission (15:32). Others appear more settled, like Philip and his four daughters in Caesarea (21:8–9). Incidentally, it is clear in 1 Corinthians 11:5 (in contrast to 14:34) that women also prophesied in Paul's churches, and Revelation 2:20 attacks a woman in Thyatira who calls herself a prophetess, labeling her a "Jezebel."

In Corinth, Paul had to struggle with people in the congregation who understood the gifts of the Spirit in a quite different way. They were enthusiasts, for whom the true mark of a Christian was the ability to speak in tongues. Paul does not deny that gift, but he insists that it is less important than prophecy and the ability to interpret tongues. Paul himself was a charismatic, but he is never called a prophet.

Finally, the Revelation to John (in the singular, even though it is a collection of revelatory visions and oracles) presents itself as a book of prophecies. In the next chapter, we will also have to look at it as an apocalyptic book, but it certainly shares some features of the prophetic style that we have been studying. John does not call himself a "prophet," except by implication, but prefers simply to be a "servant" (1:1).

By itself, this is enough evidence to show that prophecy was more important to early Christianity than we usually realize. Let us probe a little deeper, to see what that pattern has in common with the Old Testament prophets and how it differs.

The Context
of Early Christian Prophecy

The *Jewish* context is important if we are to understand what it meant to use the term "prophet" for these New Testament figures. For one thing, there was a general consensus that the days of prophecy had closed when that portion of the canon had become fixed in writing more than two centuries earlier. This view later became part of the orthodox view on the part of the rabbis, to protect their role as interpreters of the text from new revelations. A similar position developed within the church. Although there were prophetic figures who claimed to have direct revelations from God, they were rarely called prophets in Judaism of the time of Jesus. Instead, the view developed that the prophet Elijah would return at the end of times to call Israel to repent and prepare for the coming of God's Kingdom. The appearance of the prophet would be a sign that the Kingdom was about to arrive. That hope is the background for the identification of John the Baptist and of Jesus as Elijah or "the prophet."

In the *Hellenistic* world into which Paul and other Gentile missionaries moved, prophetic phenomena and oracles had a long history, but they were understood in a quite different way. For example, they were often associated with ecstatic experiences of the kind that we saw connected with the beginnings of Israelite prophecy. These experiences involved a loss of consciousness or of control over the content of the message. This is apparently the way in which the Corinthian Christians understood the gifts of the Spirit; Paul objected because their view was dividing the church rather than building up a sense of unity. Also, in the Hellenistic view, the spirit was a permanent endowment; some people by nature had this spirit, while others did not. Earlier in his letter, in 1 Corinthians 2–3, we can see Paul objecting to such a view. Both Paul and this other group agreed that the Christian life could be spirit-filled. They differed over the way in which this gift was to be understood and used.

In *the early church*, the ability to prophesy was potentially open to any Christian. In practice, however, it was apparently exercised by a limited group of individuals. In his list in 1 Corinthians 12, for example, Paul distinguishes prophets from apostles and teachers and those with other spiritual gifts, without telling us exactly how they differ. We get the impression that the boundaries between these groups are quite flexible; they have not yet crystallized into specific "offices" within the church.

Furthermore, as we noted in Acts, there were apparently two types of prophets. One type followed a Hellenistic pattern of *itinerant* prophets who had no permanent home. This pattern is vividly described in Jesus' charge to the Twelve in Matthew 10:1–16, which suggests a limited ministry to "the lost sheep of the house of Israel." Luke's version divides the charge into two parts: a temporary ministry (9:1–5) and a more permanent one among the Gentiles (10:1–12). This pattern would have made sense during the earliest days of the church, when they were expecting Jesus' return at any moment. It was appropriate to a millennialist movement of the kind we can see in passages like these. Even toward the end of the first century, we find evidence of this kind of prophet in a Christian document closely related to Matthew's Gospel, which is called the *Didache* or *The Teaching of the Twelve Apostles*. The more normal pattern, however, was that of prophets *settled* in a particular community. We see that pattern in the Corinthian church or in Caesarea, with Philip and his four daughters.

We should note one important difference from the Old Testament prophets. In early Christianity, we know of no prophets who functioned independently. To put it another way, all of their prophetic activity took place in the context of congregational worship.

Finally, we should also note that the church gradually moved to suppress prophecy. It distrusted this kind of freedom. As we might expect, the effort to limit prophecy coincided with the development of Christian law. Beginning in the middle of the second century, there was another enthusiastic, prophetic movement known generally as Montanism. However, as the church became more and more institutionalized, it found less and less place for the spirit of prophecy.

The Content
of New Testament Prophecy

The first three Gospels (called "Synoptic" because of their similar point of view) identify John the Baptist as a prophetic figure according to the Old Testament pattern. Mark's description of his physical appearance is a reminder of Elijah (in 2 Kings 1:8). Matthew 3:7–12 and Luke 3:7–18, drawing in part on a common source called "Q," give a brief summary of John's message. He condemns his audience for their behavior, calls them to repent, and pronounces God's impending judgment. The new element here is the sense of urgency, which we will see in greater detail in apocalyptic writings.

Was Jesus really a prophet? The earliest Christians thought so, but did he? We cannot know his thoughts, but we can recover a lot of what he said and did. He never calls himself a prophet. However, there are two passages in which Jesus refers to "a prophet" in a way that includes his own activity. Mark 6:4 (reported in different contexts in Matthew and Luke) says, "Prophets are not without honor, except in their hometown." Luke 13:33 is the only version of Jesus' saying, "It is impossible for a prophet to be killed outside Jerusalem." Both of these passages can be understood simply as folk sayings, but they do suggest a prophetic pattern for Jesus' ministry. In many of his sayings, Jesus reflects a sense of calling ("I came"). He speaks with a direct authority ("I say to you"), often prefacing his sayings with the word "amen" ("truly"), which has the force of an oath. His prediction of the destruction of the Temple is reported in a variety of ways in the New Testament. This is a prophetic saying, and one that played a crucial role at Jesus' trial, since it appeared to be a direct attack on the religious establishment. We must also note Jesus' symbolic actions, such as entering Jerusalem with a triumphal procession and overthrowing the tables of the money changers at the Temple. These acts are also revolutionary in the sense of challenging the authority of the Jewish leaders.

If Jesus' ministry did originally follow a prophetic form, what can we say about the content of his message? Jesus was not concerned with ceremonial purity but instead reached out to "the lost sheep," the ordinary people whose jobs would not permit them to observe all the rituals. For him, the religious leaders had lost sight of the basic demands of the Law and were focusing on peripheral matters. Jesus was not concerned with national independence, refusing to support an armed revolt against the Roman forces that occupied Jerusalem. He was concerned about the poor, the exploited, and the helpless. Yet he offered not a social and economic program but a call for religious reform. He called people back to the fundamental loyalties found in the Torah: exclusive love for God, unselfish love for one's neighbor.

What is the focus of Jesus' preaching? Clearly it is the rule (the Kingdom) of God. His preaching is as urgent as John the Baptist's, but the focus has shifted from God's judgment to God's gracious offer of a new social order. According to Jesus, that rule is about to appear in human history, and in some of his own deeds and words it is already present. Oddly enough, that "Kingdom" theme almost disappeared in the early church. Instead, they waited for the coming/return (the Parousia) of Jesus in power. Jesus himself does not describe life in the Kingdom. Instead, he tells us as his hearers how we must sacrifice everything else, how we must focus our whole lives on this one treasure, how we must be ready for its arrival at any time. Jesus continues the prophetic vision of a renewed social order, but many of his sayings have a more apocalyptic cast, which we will have to examine in the next chapter.

We get very little insight into the message of the early Christian prophets. Acts, for example, tells us only that Agabus predicted a famine (11:28) and Paul's imprisonment (21:10–11).

In 1 Corinthians 7:10–11, when he is discussing divorce, Paul appeals to a word of Jesus. He may simply be reporting a teaching of Jesus' that he has learned from other Christians. However, when he does this in other places, he usually uses the technical phrase for tradition ("I handed on to you," as in 11:23 and 15:3 of the same letter), and he also puts the divorce saying in the form of a direct command: "I give this command—not I but the Lord" (7:10). Thus this has the form of a prophetic saying. It is the risen Christ speaking through Paul.

The most obvious and most frequent use of this pattern is found in the Apocalypse (the Greek word meaning "revelation"). Virtually the entire book consists of visions and/or words that the writer receives directly from God, from Jesus, or from one of the angels. For example, in 1:10–20, John has a vision of "one like the Son of Man" who tells him to write what he sees and send it to seven churches in Asia Minor. Therefore, the letters found in chapters 2–3 are the content of his vision; they represent the risen Christ speaking to the churches through John. Essentially, the content of his message is for his readers to remain faithful in the face of the persecution and suffering that is about to happen to them. In the next chapter, I will argue that John's outlook is more that of apocalyptic than that of prophecy, so we do not need to pursue the issue here.

Many of these prophetic sayings do have the character of moral advice, either of encouragement or of warning. Generally speaking, the role of the Christian prophet is to reinforce the character of the Christian community. Like the Old Testament prophets, they present a call to moral action.[7]

These early Christian prophets played a crucial role in passing on the tradition of Jesus' sayings. If you think about it, our Gospels really contain three kinds of material. The first are authentic sayings of Jesus and narratives about events in his earthly life. A second type contains a core of authentic material, which has then been adapted to situations in the life of the church. We saw an example of this earlier in the chapter, when Luke expands the story of Jesus' sending out the twelve disciples as itinerant prophets. He adds a story of Jesus' sending out seventy, representing a mission to the Gentiles, which did not in fact happen until later in the life of the church. The third type of material consists of "sayings of the risen Jesus."[8] At first, that seems like a shocking idea because it is so unfamiliar to our way of thinking. Remember, though, that the "Great Commission" of Jesus to "Go therefore and make disciples of all nations [Gentiles]" appears in Matthew 28:18–20. They are words spoken by the risen Christ. The familiar story of the events on the road to Emmaus in Luke 24:13–49 contains a long postresurrection conversation.

For the early church, there really was no difference between the words of the earthly Jesus and those of the risen Lord. He was alive, and he continued to speak directly to the churches. The prophets were the primary group for receiving and transmitting these messages, as we saw in Revelation. No doubt the prophets were also instrumental in collecting Jesus' sayings and adapting them.

The New Testament writers are quite up front in saying that they did not really understand how to interpret the Old Testament, or the words of Jesus, until after the resurrection. This is clear in the Emmaus story, where Christ "opened their minds to understand the Scriptures" (Luke 24:45). In John's Gospel, Jesus promises that the Paraclete "will teach you everything, and remind you of all that I have said to you" (John 14:26). We can easily find other examples, but the point is that these early Christian prophets, who claimed to speak for the risen Christ, helped the early church to understand its Scriptures.

Prophetic Arguments
and Prophetic Authority

If we ask, "What reasons do these prophets give for us to accept their message?" and "Where do they get their authority?" we must give the same answer to both questions: It is the risen Lord, or the Spirit of Christ, speaking through them. The appeals or reasons they give to back up their message also explain their authority to speak.

Jesus differed from the Pharisees and other interpreters of Torah by claiming to speak on his own authority. "His teaching was direct and authoritative because it was charismatic rather than professionally learned."[9] His use of "amen" to introduce many of his sayings gave a direct, personal authority to his message.

Paul consistently called himself an apostle rather than a prophet. Yet there are many prophetic features to his life and work. In the first place, he claims that his authority comes directly from the exalted Christ. In Galatians 1:12, he insists that he did not receive his gospel from any other church leaders: "For I did not receive it from a human source, nor was I taught it, but I received it through a revelation of Jesus Christ." Similarly, in 1 Corinthians 9:1 he declares, "Am I not an apostle? Have I not seen Jesus our Lord?" In 2 Corinthians 12:1, where his authority is under attack, he speaks of "visions and revelations of the Lord," although it is not clear whether this refers to his initial contact (his "conversion") or to later experiences. In the second place, his sense of call as an apostle to the Gentiles is similar in many respects to that of the prophet Jeremiah. Paul believes that God "had set me apart before I was born" (Galatians 1:15; see Jeremiah 1:5). He believes that he has received a special commission. Third, the term "apostle" means "one who is sent"; it is the equivalent of the Old Testament concept of a messenger. In the New Testament, those who are called prophets are not pictured as messengers, but Paul describes himself again and again as an apostle, suggesting the older pattern. In this case, of course, he is a messenger or representative of Jesus Christ, to carry the gospel among the Gentiles who were not originally part of the covenant people. Finally, Paul does not hesitate to speak for Christ. In addition to the passages we have already examined, we might note 1 Corinthians 14:37: "Anyone who claims to be a prophet, or to have spiritual powers, must acknowledge that what I am writing to you is a command of the Lord."

We have already noted how John the Seer claims that his message comes from visions—for example, of Jesus Christ (Revelation 1) or of God in the heavenly council (Revelation 4–5)—or from angels, who in biblical thought are God's heavenly messengers.

In other words, the New Testament prophets also claim the authority of a direct revelation, without any human mediation. Almost always, the source of their message is the risen Christ. In many cases, the medium is a vision. All of these characteristics fit the pattern of Old Testament prophecy.

Of course, we should not be surprised to find that the early church had to struggle with false prophets. First Thessalonians is usually considered to be Paul's first letter, therefore making it the earliest piece of writing found in the New Testament. In it he encourages prophecy, but he also cautions them: "Do not quench the Spirit. Do not despise the words of the prophets, but test everything; hold fast to what is good; abstain from every form of evil" (5:19–22). First Corinthians 12–14 is Paul's effort to teach that congregation how to do things "decently and in order" (14:40), which includes subjecting the prophetic spirit to scrutiny by other prophets (14:32).

As the church grew, it had to deal with conflicting claims on the part of these prophets. Matthew 7:15–23 reflects a situation in the time when the Gospel was written. The church is to beware of false prophets. Many who confess Jesus as "Lord, Lord" and even prophesy in his name are really evildoers and will have no place in the Kingdom of Heaven, according to this Gospel. First John 4 agrees that there are many false prophets who work in the spirit of the antichrist. A simple test is whether or not they are willing to confess the humanity of Jesus, the fact that he "has come in the flesh." In the same way, John's attack on Jezebel in Revelation 2 assumes that she is a false prophet. The real issue there seems to be the degree to which the church can accommodate to its Hellenistic surroundings, since it involves eating food offered to idols. To control movements of this kind, the church moved in the direction of a more uniform set of teachings and of moral standards—in other words, toward a Christian legal tradition.

SUMMARY

Here, then, is a second pattern of moral reflection. It does not ignore the Torah or the teachings of Jesus, but it feels free to supplement those sources with insights drawn directly from an encounter with God/risen Lord/Holy Spirit. The context varies, but in the New Testament the congregation must test the prophet and his or her message. The message also varies, but essentially it calls people to be true to the vision of community set out in the Torah and in Jesus' proclamation of the Kingdom of God.

Exercise 15

Now that we have had a look at this pattern, you may want to ask yourself these questions, or discuss them in your class:

1. *What do the Old and New Testament prophets have in common? How are they different?*
2. *Do you think "law" or "prophecy" provides a more reliable basis for the Christian moral life? Why?*
3. *Should churches today encourage prophetic speaking because it can bring renewal, or should they discourage it because it can be disruptive?*

4

The Apocalyptic Demand for Religious Purity

In our ordinary conversations, the word "apocalyptic" carries with it a sense of impending doom. Whether we use it to refer to a prediction of the end of the world or the expectation of a catastrophic event (like the major earthquake that some had predicted would occur near New Madrid, Missouri, on December 3, 1990), a sense of urgency is part of the message.

Exercise 16

Suppose that you want to convince your friends and neighbors that the end of history is about to occur. What kind of language will you use? What kind of pictures and symbols help to make your point? In a group, see how many different ideas you can list.

Apocalyptic language is basically visual. It draws a picture of what is going to happen, so that even if your audience is illiterate, they will get the picture. Even more than the prophets, apocalyptic writers depend on heavenly visions and heavenly messages to dramatize their points. Think of apocalyptic literature as cartoon language. In my answer to exercise 16, I would suggest cartoons like these: a couple sitting without any oars in a rowboat that is floating toward the brink of a dam, or a train approaching a car stalled on the tracks, or a burning fuse about to reach the explosives, or the familiar mushroom cloud after a nuclear explosion. The purpose of these cartoons is not to give you information (a timetable, a detailed blueprint of what is going to happen) but to get you to do something to avoid disaster. Keep this in mind as you read the passages we will look at in this chapter.

DEFINING "APOCALYPTIC"

Several times in the last chapter I said that we would have to look again at the distinction between prophecy and apocalyptic literature. To avoid any more confusion, let us begin this chapter by defining "apocalyptic." Then we can look at some examples in the Old and New Testaments.

There is actually one other term we need to understand first. "Eschatology," from the Greek word meaning "the last" or "final," is the generic category for all teaching about "the last things." It includes such varied things as secular visions of a classless society, religious hopes for a life after death, and predictions of a nuclear catastrophe. Thus it is not tied to any particular form of hope for the future or to any particular content. "Apocalyptic," however, as we will use the term, is a subcategory of eschatology. It is a much more precise term, referring to one kind of expectation. Not all scholars use the same definition, or classify the same books as apocalyptic, but in recent years a consensus has begun to emerge. It includes three aspects: type of literature, social setting, and set of ideas.

A Type of Literature

This category refers first of all to a distinct type or genre of literature.[1] In Judaism this type of literature began to appear at the very end of the biblical period, about 200 B.C.E. This type of thinking had a significant influence on the early church, but only a few examples are included within the Bible. Within Judaism and Christianity, we have a fairly limited body of literature produced within a period of four to five hundred years.

This literary genre claims to "reveal" or "unveil" truths about God and about the fate of the readers. In fact, "revelation" is an English translation of the Greek term *apocalupsis*. One technique for unveiling is the use of visions. Another is the use of exotic symbols (heavenly creatures, hybrid animals, cataclysmic battles) and code words. These symbols have a hidden meaning for the initiated, so that the author can comment, "He who has an ear, let him hear what the Spirit says to the churches" (a refrain in Revelation 2–3) or "Let the reader understand." Many apocalyptic documents are written under an assumed name, usually a famous figure of the past (Ezra, Baruch, Enoch, Paul, the Virgin Mary). Often the ancient figure predicts current events in the form of a vision or a prophecy.

The Social Setting

These writings almost always address a group facing a crisis: the destruction of the Temple, 66–70 c.e.; persecution, actual or threatened; a struggle to maintain the purity of the faith in a world of secular values. The exotic symbolism helps to provide the group with a sense of identity. If you know what is about to happen, you can get closer to others in the group and help one another resist the forces that threaten you.

Apocalyptic writings, therefore, are sectarian. Modern sociologists use the term "sect" in at least two different ways. One describes a group that has separated itself from the larger society. Another describes a community (usually a religious one) that has split off from a larger, parent group and feels somewhat isolated. We can find examples of both types of sectarian communities in the late Jewish and early Christian apocalyptic literature.

A Set of Ideas

Most older definitions focused on apocalyptic as a theology or an ideology (a set of ideas). To a great extent, this is what makes it different from other kinds of eschatology. For example, in this literature we usually find a sharp *dualism* between this world and a new one to come in the near future. This world is in the hands of evil powers and must be destroyed. Then God will create a new world, in which sorrow and suffering will no longer exist. Linked with that idea is a strong *pessimism* about life in this world. Things have become so corrupt that there is no longer any hope of turning things around. God will destroy the world as we know it, and then create a better one. Of course, if you remain faithful to God in this corrupt age, you can expect to be rewarded by sharing in the life of the age to come. In the biblical tradition, the idea of a resurrection of the dead is clearly stated for the first time in this apocalyptic literature. This idea helps to explain how the faithful who have died can share in the new age: God will raise them from death to new life.

One important difference between prophecy and apocalyptic lies in this set of ideas. Prophecy is this-worldly. It says that God will bring human history to its promised fulfillment. God's Kingdom will be on this earth. The Messiah is a figure (human or divine) who will establish justice and righteousness and peace in this world. Apocalyptic, in contrast, gives up on this world. It shifts God's victory to a cosmic level, to a new world or a new age that stands in sharp contrast to the one we know. Today, most popular Christian views of "heaven" are otherworldly, even if they no longer carry a sense of urgency about its coming.

Here, then, are three pieces of a definition of "apocalyptic." It is a specific type of literature, usually written for a sectarian community, that expresses a distinct point of view about God's role in future events. Now we need to turn our attention to some examples within Scripture.

APOCALYPTIC IN ISRAEL

Again, we will consider the context of this type of literature before looking at its content or major themes.

The Context of Apocalyptic

How and why did this type of literature emerge within Judaism? One approach finds the answers in external factors, particularly the influence of Persian religion on the Israelites during and after the period of the Exile. That religion understood the world dualistically as a conflict between good and evil, between light and darkness. However, a second approach, which has been more popular recently, sees the rise of apocalyptic primarily as a result of conflicts within Judaism itself after the rebuilding of the Temple. As some of the older priestly groups were displaced, they became disillusioned and began to hope that God would intervene and reverse Israel's fortunes.[2] In fact, these explanations are not mutually exclusive; the truth probably lies in some combination of factors.

For the period that concerns us, we should keep two things in mind. First, "apocalypticism" was not an organized social movement. It did not develop its own structure and leadership, in contrast to the Pharisees. Second, it was a fairly widespread attitude at the time when Christianity emerged. It provided the context for the messages of John the Baptist, Jesus, Paul, and much of early Christianity.

Exercise 17

The best examples of this type of literature in the Old Testament are found in Isaiah 24–27 and 61–66, Zechariah 9–14, and Daniel. We will look at only one of those examples, the one that is probably the most familiar one. Read Daniel 7–12. *If you have time, read chapters 1–6 as well.*

1. *Look for passages that fit one or more of the characteristics of apocalyptic.*
2. *Ask yourself what the author of this book was trying to convey to his readers.*

One historical crisis contributing to the rise of apocalyptic occurred in 168 B.C.E., when Israel was invaded by the Syrian (Seleucid) ruler Antiochus IV, often called Epiphanes because he claimed to be a "manifest" form of the Greek god Zeus. He plundered the sacred Temple, prevented Jews from offering sacrifices there any more, and set up a statue of Zeus in its innermost sanctuary (the "holy of holies"). This event is mentioned in "code language" in Daniel 11:31 and 12:11 as "the abomination that makes desolate." Antiochus also tried to force Greek language and culture on the Jews. To enforce this policy, he ordered that a woman whose child had been circumcised be killed with her child hung around her neck, and he made it a crime to have a copy of the Torah. Antiochus's policy of persecuting the Jews triggered a revolt known as the Maccabean revolution. This succeeded in liberating the Temple in 165 B.C.E., three years to the day after it had been profaned, and established a period of Jewish independence from foreign rule. The victory is celebrated in the Jewish festival of Hanukkah.

Daniel was written during this period of conflict and persecution. The date of writing can be pinpointed to 166–165 B.C.E., making it the last book of the Old Testament to be composed. Although the book claims to be set in the ancient Persian empire, the author's knowledge of that period is often confused, while it gets more accurate as he moves toward his own time. On the other hand, when he predicts events that will happen after 165, he is simply wrong. The obvious conclusion is that he wrote before the outcome of the conflict was clear.

From a literary point of view, the book consists of two parts. The first half (chapters 1–6), a collection of stories about Daniel, is a piece of historical fiction. The second half is a collection of four visions (chapters 7, 8, 9, and 10–12). Most of the apocalyptic material is found here. How many characteristics of apocalyptic literature did you find when you did the exercise?

The Content
of the Apocalyptic Message

One obvious theme running through these chapters is that of *conflict*. Through his visions, Daniel describes four kingdoms whose kings ruthlessly set out to conquer the earth, a process in the Middle East that has had some interesting parallels in recent years. The picture of them rising from the sea in Daniel 7 is a vivid reminder of a myth that represents the sea as the source of all chaos.[3] The vision in chapters 10–12 focuses on the actions of Antiochus; in these chapters we discover that the conflict on earth is a reflection of one being fought at a cosmic or supernatural level. Michael, the prince of angels, is fighting against the "princes" of the other nations (10:12–14, 20–21; see also 8:25). Thus, ultimately, the real conflict is between Israel's God and others who claim to have divine power. This notion of a cosmic conflict, as we noted earlier, is one that distinguishes apocalyptic from prophecy.

Reading carefully, we can see that the Israelites are suffering as a result of this conflict. Indeed, the author warns his readers that the worst is yet to come. They must prepare themselves for a final tribulation, for a climax of suffering in the days just before the end of the world as we know it (12:1).

In the face of such threats, the author urges his readers to be *faithful*. They must resist the temptation to break their covenant with God in the face of persecution. If they do, they will be considered wise (11:32–35). They must *purify* themselves (12:10). The conduct the author expects is not any different from that demanded by the Law and the prophets (9:4, 10). In fact, the long prayer of Daniel in chapter 9, which interrupts the visions, is both a confession and a prophetic appeal for the people to repent. Notice how the themes of law, prophecy, and wisdom all come together in this apocalyptic book. What makes this book different, then, is not the type of conduct required. What is new is not the content of the message but rather the sense of urgency that we noticed at the beginning of this chapter.

The faithful community, according to Daniel, protects itself from the outside world by observing the covenant demands. In chapters 1–6, the author tells the story of some role models. Shadrach, Meshach, and Abednego are thrown into the fiery furnace because they refuse to worship a graven image (chapter 3). Daniel is thrown to the lions because he defies a governmental prohibition and continues to pray faithfully to his god (chapter 6). If the Jews suffering under Antiochus will only follow the example of these heroes, they will become a community set apart from the rest of the world by their faithfulness and their purity. They will be a sectarian community.

The Arguments for Purity

Why should Daniel's readers resist persecution, when they could easily give in to the demands of this foreign ruler? Why should they keep their identity and their purity when it only meant more suffering? This was the first time in their history that the Jews were persecuted simply for their religion, but unfortunately it was not the last. Their example has inspired Christians and people of other faiths who have shared this experience of persecution. What arguments does the author of Daniel give to support his call to faithfulness?

On the one hand, there is the threat of God's *judgment*. This is not developed in Daniel to the same extent that it appears in other apocalyptic literature, but it is present in the picture of God as the cosmic ruler (chapter 7), as "the Ancient of Days." God, through the angelic forces, will ultimately conquer all those who refuse to acknowledge God's rule.

On the positive side, Daniel focuses on the *promise* of new life for those who remain faithful. Just as God protected Daniel and Shadrach and his friends in their earthly trials, so God will deliver those whose names are written in "the book," including some who have died and will be resurrected (12:1–4). At God's judgment the saints will receive the kingdom (7:18, 22, 27), even though Daniel does not tell us what this kingdom involves.

One of the most difficult problems in Daniel is to know what he meant by "one like a son of man" (7:13, RSV). It has focused the attention of scholars because so many of Jesus' sayings use the same image, most often referring to a heavenly figure who will appear and carry out God's judgment. In this passage it does not have that meaning. Does it refer to an individual at all, or is this "Son of Man" a symbol for the "saints of the Most High," since both of them are given dominion by God? If it is an individual, does the term refer to an angelic figure, probably Michael, or does it anticipate a Christlike figure? One thing is certain: It represents God's ultimate victory over the forces of evil, when the faithful will be rewarded by sharing in God's rule.

Apocalyptic Authority

In Daniel, as in the prophetic books we have examined, visions and dreams provide the authority for the author's message. These represent the direct revelation of God's plan for the future. Interestingly enough, in chapters 1–6, Daniel is the one who interprets the dreams. In the last half of the book, he has the dreams, and an angel interprets for him. Chapter 7 acts as a transition in the book. In it, the author stands in the heavenly court and learns about God's judgment and God's promise. In other apocalyptic writings, the author is taken on a secret journey in order to gain some esoteric knowledge.

Near the end of his visions, Daniel is told to seal the book, "until the time of the end" (12:4). This suggests that his message is complete, not that the book is to be hidden away. "It is true that the perspective conveyed in the vision is not publicly accessible but requires special, apocalyptic revelation. Yet the whole purpose of this revelation, in the case of Daniel, is to make the masses understand."[4]

Finally, prayer is another means by which Daniel not only communicates directly with God but also receives wisdom from the angel Gabriel (9:22). Daniel's call to faithfulness and purity, therefore, is spoken with a divine authority.

APOCALYPTIC IN EARLY CHRISTIANITY

In order to appreciate the significance of apocalyptic in early Christianity, we need to look at the context in which it developed.

The Context

As we have already noted, Christianity emerged in a Jewish environment in which apocalyptic hopes were a major element.

Indeed, because the first Christians awaited Jesus' *Parousia* or "coming" within their own lifetime,[5] we can best understand Jesus' followers as an apocalyptic or millenarian movement. In 1 Thessalonians, probably the first Christian writing to survive, Paul paints a strange picture of Christ ("the Lord") descending from heaven, of the dead rising first, and of those who are still alive rising through the air to meet him (4:15–18). Similarly, 1 Corinthians 15:52 is a passage often heard at funeral services without grasping its original meaning. Paul asserts, "The dead will be raised imperishable, and we [those in his audience] will be changed." Elsewhere in the same letter, he answers their questions about sex and marriage with the qualification "The appointed time has grown short" (7:29).

Can this sense of urgency be traced back to Jesus himself? Certainly one strand of his message emphasized this. Many parables tell us that we should be ready for God's rule to arrive at any moment, when we least expect it. Mark 9:1 records Jesus as saying, "There are some standing here who will not taste death until they see that the kingdom of God come with power." Since events did not turn out as Jesus predicted, this saying must be authentic. Jesus' words at the Last Supper are reported in several different versions, but each version refers to a fulfillment in the immediate future. Finally, many of Jesus' sayings imply that the "Son of Man" will appear soon. It was only natural that the early church identified Jesus as the Son of Man and awaited his coming. There is, of course, another side to Jesus' message that points to signs of fulfillment within his own ministry, but the apocalyptic element is certainly present, as it is in the message of John the Baptist.

Even though it took shape in this kind of environment, the early church actually produced very little apocalyptic literature. There is a brief example in 2 Thessalonians 2:3–10, which is so different from the passage in 1 Thessalonians that many people question whether Paul actually wrote it. Similarly, Mark 13 is often called "the Little Apocalypse" because of its scheme of events that will occur before the end. Many of these sayings stand in tension with Jesus' insistence that we cannot know when the kingdom will arrive, so it is likely that this chapter shows signs of editing by the early church.

The best example of early Christian apocalyptic is the book of Revelation, so we will focus our attention on it. It fits all of our criteria for this literary genre, even though it is unique in having the author identify himself. As we have seen, the author preferred to speak about prophecy. When we classify it as apocalyptic, we are using a modern category but a more accurate one.

John, the visionary and author of the book, says that he was on the island of Patmos in the eastern Mediterranean "because of the word of God and the testimony of Jesus" (1:9). The implication is that he is an exile or prisoner. His book is directed to the seven churches in Asia Minor that are addressed in chapters 2–3. Even a quick look at the book shows that it is written for people facing persecution. However, John is more concerned with the threat of persecution than with its actual presence; and there is no evidence that the persecution is a result of an official policy of the Roman authorities. For those two reasons, there is no need to accept the traditional dating of the book either during the reign of Nero (c. 65 C.E.) or of the emperor Domitian (c. 95 C.E.); it could have been written any time during the second half of the first Christian century.

The structure of the book is confusing. After his narrative introduction, John reports a vision of "one like the Son of Man," who is obviously the risen Christ (1:13). From him, John receives the message that he delivers to the seven churches (chapters 2–3). Next, John is taken into the heavenly court in a scene that reminds us of the call of Isaiah (Isaiah 6). Here he sees and hears the praise offered to God and to Christ, the Lion/Lamb who is the only one able to open the seven seals of the scroll containing the secrets about the future (Revelation 4–5). The visions that follow consist basically of cycles of seven. This pattern is most obvious in the seven seals (chapters 6–7), the seven trumpets (chapters 8–11), and the seven bowls or plagues (chapters 15–16), but even in these cases there are interludes. Originally there may have been seven cycles of seven visions each. Some commentators can still discover that pattern, but only by forcing it onto the material. There is a description of the dragon and the beast (chapters 12–13, with echoes of Daniel), of the deliverance of the saints (chapter 14), of the destruction of Babylon (chapters 17–18; probably a code name for Rome), of the marriage ceremony of the Lamb (chapter 19), and of the final victory of Christ and God over all the forces of evil (chapters 19–20). The book concludes with a triumphant vision of a new heaven and new earth and a new Jerusalem (21:1–22:5) and a narrative section (22:6–21).

Keep two things in mind as you read Revelation. First, this is symbolic, picture language that is not meant to be taken literally. The dragon stands for chaos, in the way that Uncle Sam represents the United States. John likes to contrast images. The lion of Judah becomes the Lamb who was slain and who rose to conquer (chapter 5). The woman threatened by the dragon in chapter 12 probably stands for the church, although she could also refer to Judaism, while in chapters 17–18 Babylon/Rome is pictured as a whore for worshiping other gods (an image used for Israel by Hosea). The city of Babylon epitomizes corruption, while Jerusalem represents the final hope for life with God.

Second, John's message was intended for Christians of his time, for the churches of Asia Minor in the last half of the first century. He was not preparing a blueprint or a timetable for later generations, so we should not try to find allusions to current events in his book. Much Christian energy has been wasted trying to date the millennial rule of Christ and his followers. This image occupies only three verses in the whole of Scripture. The context makes it clear that the millennial rule is a special reward promised for Christian martyrs. To use it as a chronological scheme for world history is to misunderstand not only these verses but also the rest of the New Testament hope for the future. What, then, do John's visions have to say to the churches?

Exercise 18

Read Revelation 1–5, 14, 20–22. Of course, if you have time, read through the entire book.

1. *See how many characteristics of apocalyptic you can find in these chapters. Are they the same as the ones you found in Daniel?*
2. *In the letters to the seven churches (chapters 2–3), notice that there is a formula that introduces and concludes each letter. Then list the things for which each church is* praised *and/or* blamed.
3. *In 14:1–5 (and earlier in 7:1–8), John singles out 144,000 for special praise. What have they done to deserve it?*
4. *In your own words, what kind of behavior does John expect from his readers?*

The Content of John's Revelation

Even more than Daniel, John describes *conflict*; it is an essential part of his visions, especially in chapters 6–20. The extent of the destruction is almost overwhelming: a quarter of the earth from famine and pestilence (6:8); a third of the earth, sea creatures, and sky, plus fresh water pollution (chapter 8); a third of humanity following five months of torture (chapter 9); seven thousand in an earthquake (11:13); the seven plagues and devastation of Babylon (chapters 16–18). As in Daniel, this is ultimately a conflict with the unseen powers of evil. Satan will be defeated (20:7–10), and finally Death and Hades (20:14). These images rival any modern pictures of the effects of a nuclear holocaust. John is not trying to lead us step by step through a series of events between now and the end of the world. Rather, he multiplies the images of violence so that we will resist every challenge that might weaken our faith.

The unfortunate aspect of John's message is that the conflict is almost exclusively good versus bad, us versus them. Antipas has already died (2:13), and other Christians will face martyrdom in the future (6:9–11 and 20:4, apparently in addition to the 144,000 in 14:1–5). Apart from this, virtually everyone who suffers and dies is an enemy of God, and by definition this means an enemy of the church as well.

However, John never guarantees that we are the winners, the saints. There are some things we must do if we want to be counted in that company. John dramatizes the conflict to strengthen the sense of community among those who hear and read his message.

In the letters to the seven churches, there are two key terms. One is *endurance*, often qualified with "faithful" or "patient" even when that adjective does not appear in the Greek text. "This does not refer to a general patience amid the problems and adversities of life, but iron resistance in the face of trials and tribulations that arise when one confesses Jesus Christ . . . . "[6] The other is *witness*, which in Greek is the stem for our word "martyr." The primary meaning is not to give your life but rather to remain faithful. Together, then, these two words summarize the response John expects from his readers, in the face of the conflict he describes.

If you were living in one of John's communities in Ephesus or Smyrna or Pergamum or one of the other seven cities, the point of John's letter was perfectly clear. You could not worship at any of the temples in your city. You should avoid taking part in any ceremonies or rituals or practices that might compromise your faith in any way. That is why John attacks eating food offered to idols and practicing immorality (2:14).[7]

Even more, you should avoid contact with other Christians who seem willing to compromise their faith, particularly false prophets (2:20; also 19:20 and 20:10). This would include the Jezebel (2:20–24), the Nicolaitans (2:6, 15), and the "teaching of Balaam" (2:14). These names are part of John's code language for rival Christian groups. "The conflict is not really over immorality and the eating of sacrificial meat alone, but over the stance toward cultural and religious accommodation which these practices symbolize."[8]

John's moral strategy, therefore, is a call for *purity*. It is a sectarian ethic, a call for a religious counterculture. This is why he warns the Christians living in Babylon: "Come out of her, my people, so that you do not take part in her sins, and so that you do not share in her plagues" (18:4). Apart from endurance and witness, however, it is hard to know exactly what this purity involves. John does say that the saints "keep the commandments of God and hold fast to the faith of Jesus" (14:12), but nothing else in the book suggests ceremonial behavior or a strict interpretation of the Law. Even when the seven churches are praised, it is for very general behavior: for their works, for their faith and service, for their endurance, for holding fast the faith. There are no parables, no lists of virtues and vices, no specific instructions of the kind we find in Paul's letters. One exception is the statement in 14:4 that the 144,000 "have not defiled themselves with women, for they are virgins." Taken literally, it suggests celibacy as a requirement for a select group of Christians. However, it may simply be a symbolic way of speaking about the importance of keeping the purity of their faith. In any case, it does reinforce the sense that John's churches must be a breed apart, in their faithfulness and in their living. Otherwise, John gives little specific content to the moral life.

John's Arguments for Purity

One reason why we should endure and keep pure, according to John, is to avoid divine *judgment* (22:12). John makes this point not in the form of a logical argument but by multiplying images for God's *power*. God is the cosmic ruler, the Alpha and Omega, but God shares this power with the heavenly messengers and particularly with the Lamb, who becomes the ruler of the kings of the earth (1:5; 19:15). The "godless" will be eliminated. All who refuse to accept God's sovereignty will be destroyed. Surprisingly, most of the destruction in Revelation is not caused by worldly rulers; it is a result of God's action. It is announced, or carried out, by the angels. Taken literally, this picture of God as a ruthless, vengeful warrior is not very attractive except to people who feel oppressed and helpless. The real purpose of John's imagery, however, is to strengthen the community of faith. Remember that we are different from the rest of the world, John reminds us. If we lose what is distinctive about our faith, if we assimilate to what the world expects, we are as good as dead.

The positive aspect of his message, of course, is the *promise of uninterrupted life* in God's presence. The saints, those who endure and remain pure, will share in God's rule and will sing God's praises. Recall the promises to those churches that conquer: food from the tree of life (2:7), the crown of life (2:10), hidden manna and a white stone (2:17), power over the nations and a white star (2:26–28), white garments and their names permanently inscribed in the book of life (3:5), a pillar in the temple (3:12), and a seat on God's throne (3:21). This collage of symbols, most of them drawn from the Old Testament, promises victory to the faithful. The 144,000 is not a fixed number but a symbol that Israel's hopes will be fulfilled (7:1–8); they are joined by a larger number who survive the "great ordeal" (7:9–14). To use a crude analogy, John's book is a pep talk: "Keep yourself pure. Be a winner."

The Authority of John's Revelation

The source of John's authority is clear. It comes directly from God (chapters 4–5), from the risen Christ (chapter 1), or from angelic messengers (most of the other visions). John stands in this chain of authority when he sends his message to the angels of the seven churches, which apparently represent something like guardian angels.

The ways in which he receives these messages (visions, auditions, etc.) should be familiar by now, so that we do not need to elaborate on them. In contrast to Daniel, John is told not to seal up the book, because "the time is near" (22:10); and he also warns others not to add anything to it (22:18–19).

At a more practical level, however, John does not claim any direct authority over the churches. He is much more reluctant than Paul to tell them what to do. He refers to himself as a "servant" (1:1) and as "your brother" (1:9). Even the angel in 19:10 and 22:9 is called a "fellow servant." The churches seem to be organized in a nonhierarchical way; there is no clear structure of leadership. This is exactly what we would expect to find in a charismatic, apocalyptic sect. John's authority, then, lies in the visions themselves.

Exercise 19

1. What do you find most attractive about this approach to the moral life? Least attractive?
2. The sense of urgency, of the nearness of the end, is central to apocalyptic imagery. What place, if any, should that play in Christian preaching and teaching today?

5

Wisdom as a Guide to the Moral Life

What does the term "wisdom" mean to you? We do not usually associate it with the kind of technical knowledge that occupies the self-help sections of the local bookstores: home repair and auto mechanic manuals, craft instruction, or folklore of the kind popularized in the *Foxfire* books. Occasionally we speak about a practical or folk wisdom of the kind found in Aesop's fables, Ann Landers's advice columns, and popular authors like Dale Carnegie, Norman Vincent Peale, and Robert Fulghum. Usually, however, we reserve the term "wisdom" for something more than a normal education. The wise person has a special kind of insight, gained from experience and reflection.

Exercise 20

1. *Think of people or books that you consider to have or display "wisdom." What qualities do they have? What have you learned from them?*
2. *Then think of any characters or books in the Bible that have the same qualities, or from which you can learn the same kind of lessons.*

WISDOM IN ISRAEL

There was a long tradition of wisdom teaching in the Ancient Near East, so it is not surprising that we find evidence of the same kind of material in the Old Testament. Proverbs 22:17–23:11, for example, is copied almost word for word from a wisdom book of Pharaoh Amenemope. Occasionally this lore consists of technical knowledge, especially among craftsmen and farmers, or of proverbial sayings like our familiar "A stitch in time saves nine." More often, however, it refers to the other two types of material that we have already mentioned: practical teaching about how to lead a good life and philosophical or reflective literature. In the Old Testament, we find examples of the practical type in Proverbs, Ecclesiastes, and some Psalms; all of these belong to the "Writings," the last part of the Hebrew Bible to be collected and accepted as Scripture. The best example of the philosophical type, of course, is the book of Job, but because of its length and complexity we will not consider it here. The Apocrypha consists of other late Jewish writings, which are not included within the Jewish or Protestant canon but are accepted as canonical in the Roman Catholic and Orthodox traditions. Two important works in the Apocrypha shed important light on the development of the Jewish wisdom literature (or "Wisdom," for short) and were familiar to many New Testament writers: the Wisdom of Solomon and Ecclesiasticus, also called Ben Sira or Sirach.

The Context of Wisdom Literature

The wisdom tradition in Israel is traced back to Solomon; Proverbs, Ecclesiastes, and the Wisdom of Solomon are attributed to him. Apparently there were two stages in its development. The earliest one, during the period of the monarchy, consisted of a group of sages who served as advisers to the king. Jeremiah 18:18 identifies three groups and their responsibility or authority: "for instruction [i.e., Torah] shall not perish from the priest, nor counsel from the wise, nor the word from the prophet." Jeremiah criticizes the wise men for having failed to hear God's word, and perhaps also for having neglected the Torah (9:12–16). We do not have much direct information about who this group of wise men were or what they did, but foreign policy was almost certainly an area in which their advice brought them into conflict with the prophets.

With the Exile and the collapse of the monarchy, the wisdom tradition was increasingly taken over by the priests, until in Sirach wisdom means studying the Torah and keeping the commandments. The wise men are the scholars, the scribes.

Within the wisdom literature, we will focus primarily on proverbial sayings. In addition to proverbs, we can find such literary forms as the long poem (the body of the book of Job), parable, allegory, fable, riddle, hymn, and prayer and grouping by numbers (for example, sets of threes or fours). Like the Psalms, much of the wisdom literature consists of poetry. It uses the style of parallelism, in which the idea of one line is repeated in the next to strengthen, modify, or contrast with the original.

The Content of Wisdom Teaching

Exercise 21

Read Proverbs 1–3, 5, 8, 14–15, 22–24 (which includes the material borrowed from Egypt), and Ecclesiastes 1–3. Browse through the other chapters in those books if you have time. Ask yourself:

1. *What kinds of issues concern these writers? What advice do they give?*
2. *What arguments do they use to encourage people to pursue wisdom?*

Most of these chapters deal with questions of practical wisdom, that is, how to live the good life. Just think about what is missing in this literature. There is no focus on God's active presence in historical events, or on God's exclusive covenant with Israel, or on the promise of a life beyond death. Instead, the focus is on life in this world, usually on the individual rather than the covenant community. It is similar in many ways to recent philosophical trends such as existentialism and humanism. The whole mood and tone of this literature is different from what we have considered so far. One writer emphasizes its uniqueness in these words:

> It occupies, indeed, an entirely unique position, for whereas the other types are all firmly rooted in the specific religious tradition of Israel and are concerned exclusively with its life and institutions, the wisdom books say nothing whatever about Israel, its history and political vicissitudes, its peculiar status as the people of God, its cult, laws, priesthood, or prophets.[1]

Proverbs is really a compilation of material composed over a long period of time, as some of the headings indicate (chapters 25, 30, 31). The most recent material is found in chapters 1–9, where wisdom is linked to "the fear of the Lord" and the advice is addressed to "my son." Ecclesiastes, on the other hand, is a self-conscious literary composition by a single author.

Here are some of the themes in the chapters suggested for reading in Exercise 21. Compare them with your own list.

The wise person *exercises self-control* or *discipline*: "Whoever loves discipline loves knowledge" (12:1). Sometimes this is referred to as "the Lord's" discipline (3:11–12), but more often it means listening to your parents (see 1:8) or your teachers (5:12–13). To be wise means to act cautiously and with discretion (14:16–17). It means controlling your anger (14:29; 15:18). To be wise means to follow the path or the way set for you by God (3:17; 20:24). It means to be honest, industrious, and patient. Examples apply this advice to life within the family, to sexual relations, to business, and to politics. In that sense, the wisdom literature, just like the Torah, includes all of life.

The wise person *avoids foolish behavior*. That sounds redundant, but over and over these proverbs use the contrast between wise and foolish persons to tell you what *not* to do. It isn't smart, Proverbs tells us, to commit adultery or patronize a prostitute (for example, see portions of chapters 2, 5, 7, 9), to gossip (10:19), to be a glutton (23:20–21) or a drunkard (23:29–35, a vivid description by someone who apparently knew what he was writing about!). The saying about gossiping is reflected in the posters prominent during World War II that warned "Loose lips cost lives." Foolish behavior leads to destruction or to Sheol, a place of permanent oblivion.

In Ecclesiastes, we find a heavy dose of *skepticism*, a theme very different from what we have encountered so far. The familiar passage that begins "For everything there is a season" (3:1–9), popularized during the '60s in the song "Turn, Turn, Turn," really suggests that the important events in our lives are out of our control. Furthermore, the author suggests, God cannot really be known (3:10–15, especially the claim that "[God] has put a sense of past and future into their minds, yet they cannot find out what God has done from the beginning to the end"). This life is all there is; death cancels everything (2:16; 3:18–22). What a far cry this is from Isaiah's affirmation that God is the Creator and Redeemer of the world. Life for this preacher (who is also called Koheleth) is essentially a mystery.

In some passages in Proverbs, we meet for the first time *Wisdom personified*. She takes on a life of her own, as the mind or intelligence of God that is present in the created order (3:19–20). In 8:22–31, this Wisdom is identified as the first of God's created acts, who participated with God in the rest of creation.[2] We have here the female counterpart of the idea of God's Logos or Word, which appears in the beginning of John's Gospel. Whether or not it began for this reason, one result of this speculation about the personification of Wisdom was to make the goddesses of other religions less attractive. In Proverbs, Wisdom assumes a separate identity, but she is God's creature and not a rival divine figure.

Arguments for the Good Life

We expect to be told that we should value wisdom for its own sake, but instead the rationale in this literature is what we usually call instrumental or pragmatic. We should desire wisdom because it is a means to the good life. It will bring us happiness, long life, riches, honor, pleasantness, and peace (3:13–18). Proverbs suggests a simple equation. Wisdom brings worldly prosperity and success, while foolishness brings suffering and failure. That simple equation is challenged in Ecclesiastes and even more in Job, so it is not a characteristic of wisdom literature as a whole.

A second appeal is to principles of righteousness, justice, and equity (for example, 1:3; 2:9; 21:3; 22:8). We should value wisdom because it will help us to understand how to deal with other people: rich and poor, king and subject, neighbors and strangers. Wisdom is the key to proper social relationships.

A final appeal, which appears most often in the latest material (chapters 1–9), is to "the fear of the Lord" or the "knowledge" of God. "The fear of the Lord is the beginning of wisdom, and the knowledge of the Holy One is insight" (9:10). "Fear," of course, means awe or respect. Interestingly enough, though, we do not hear anything about the sacrificial system and the cultic requirements that play such a large role in the Torah.

Authority in the Wisdom Tradition

Authority in the wisdom tradition is grounded in human reason. Even though our reason is a gift from God, it is a gift that we share with all human beings, whether or not they belong to the covenant community. The same insights are available to everyone. Wisdom is human-centered and this-worldly. It does not deny God, but it does not try very hard to explore the mystery of God's existence. Those Christians today who think that all humanism is secular need to read this wisdom literature more carefully, because what we find here is a theological humanism.

In contrast to the Torah, Wisdom does not appeal to a code of laws given in ages past, which we must interpret and apply to modern problems. In contrast to prophecy and apocalyptic, Wisdom does not appeal to an immediate, direct revelation from God. The wisdom teachers remain relatively anonymous, at least when compared to the prophets. We do not need to know who wrote or collected these proverbs, because the authority lies in the message and not in the person. We accept its authority when the message helps us to understand how human relationships work.

WISDOM IN EARLY CHRISTIANITY

It is no surprise that we do not find a strong wisdom tradition in the early church. The initial enthusiasm and apocalyptic hopes, the demands of spreading the gospel and organizing new churches, the continuing task of working out a new church discipline—all left very little time for reflection. Nevertheless, the wisdom tradition did influence the New Testament writings.

A New Context

We can identify at least three trends in the period just before and during the rise of Christianity. The first was the growing tendency to identify the content of Wisdom with that of the Torah, which we have already seen. Second, the spread of Greek language and culture produced a hybrid or syncretism of ideas that we call Hellenistic Judaism. Many of the first churches emerged from synagogues reflecting this type of thinking, such as the Hellenists mentioned in Acts 7. Speculation about Wisdom as a separate being flourished in these circles. Third, as Paul and other Christian missionaries founded churches in Asia Minor and Europe, a different kind of wisdom had an impact on Christianity in the form of popular Greek philosophy. We will look briefly at an example of each of these trends as it appears in the New Testament.

The Content of Wisdom Teaching

Exercise 22

Read James again, paying special attention to chapters 1 and 3. Look for passages where the author talks about wisdom. Also look for examples of wisdom teaching of the kind we saw in Proverbs.

James is basically a Jewish-Christian writing. We are not surprised, then, to find references to wisdom alongside James's use of the Law. For him, the connection between wisdom and law is very practical and not at all abstract. There are four explicit references to wisdom, one in 1:5 (where it is a gift from God) and the rest in 3:13–18. There is a clear citation of Proverbs 3:34 in James 4:6–7, and there are possible allusions to wisdom writings in 1:5, 3:18, 4:13, and 5:6. In addition, however, many of the themes in James reflect those that we found in the Old Testament.

James focuses on several issues of *personal morality*. The first of these is the need to *endure* in the face of trials (1:2–4, 14–15). The language is the same that we found in the Apocalypse, but here the meaning is different. "Trials" refers to personal temptations, not to persecution by outsiders. A second theme that runs through this epistle is the need to *control your tongue*. It involves controlling your anger (1:19–21), putting a rein or bridle on your tongue as a mark of true religion (1:26), avoiding slander (4:11–12), and refusing to boast (3:14; 4:13–17) or to take an oath (5:12). Teaching, which is one way of passing on the wisdom tradition, is risky because it may involve imperfect speech (3:2). This is followed by several metaphors that illustrate the dangers of gossip and cursing (3:3–12). This kind of self-control is important, because slander can harm another Christian (1:11), and gossip is like a fire that can destroy a whole forest (3:5). We can spot a third theme in the *warnings against double-mindedness*, which reminds us of Jesus' saying in the Sermon on the Mount about trying to serve two masters. If you are such a person, you receive nothing from God and do not know how to pray with faith (1:6–8). Double-mindedness is linked to friendship with the world (4:4) and with the devil (4:7). The comment that we can use the same tongue to praise God and curse other people (3:9–12) is a similar thought.

There are also several examples of *social morality*. We have already looked at James's use of the Law and of the command to "love your neighbor." A major issue in James is the contrast between rich and poor, and the author *warns against favoritism* toward the rich. Some readers see a split within the community for which James was writing, but it makes better sense to see the rich as outsiders who oppress the Christians, drag them into court, and blaspheme their good name (that is, their name as Christians, not their personal reputations; 2:6–7 and 5:1–6). It is not clear in 2:1–4 whether the community had actually bowed and scraped when a rich man came to worship, but James obviously says to avoid that kind of behavior. Finally, there are a number of *warnings against conflict*, but these are not linked directly to wisdom material. Social evils such as war and conflict have their roots in the lack of self-discipline, particularly the inability to control your own desires (1:15; 4:1).

In addition to this type of practical wisdom that we find in James, we find a striking use of speculative wisdom in Paul's letters. Basically, Paul argues that Jesus Christ is the Wisdom of God. Christ performs all the functions that Wisdom did in Jewish thought. Christ existed with God before creation. He knew and carried out God's purpose for creation. God sent him to reveal that purpose and to redeem the world. In 1 Corinthians 1:18–25, Paul explicitly says that the cross is the center of the Christian faith because it shows us that Christ is the power of God and the Wisdom of God. That insight leads Paul to develop his moral teaching in different ways, some of which we will look at in the next chapter. He is not very much interested in the practical wisdom that we saw in Proverbs and James.

A third pattern is the direct influence of Hellenistic popular philosophy. We find several kinds of moral exhortation or advice in the New Testament. Much of it is drawn from the popular wisdom of the time and given a Christian veneer. This material differs in form from the Jewish wisdom literature, but not necessarily in its content.

One type of practical wisdom is found in *lists of vices and virtues*. Galatians 5:19–23 is an excellent example. Paul identifies "the works of the flesh" as "fornication, impurity, licentiousness, idolatry, sorcery, enmities, strife, jealousy, anger, quarrels, dissensions, factions, envy, drunkenness, carousing, and things like these." He then contrasts this list with "the fruit of the Spirit": "love, joy, peace, patience, kindness, generosity, faithfulness, gentleness, and self-control." Although several of Paul's favorite words appear in the second list, there is nothing peculiarly Christian about this vision of the good life; common sense could lead you to conclude which is the better way to live. We find a similar list in Colossians 3:5–8, 12–14, where the contrast is between the old earthly nature, to which we should have died, and the new life in Christ. Other examples list only vices: Romans 1:29–31; 1 Corinthians 6:9–10; Ephesians 4:31; 1 Timothy 1:9–10; 2 Timothy 3:2–4; 1 Peter 2:1 and 4:3. The point here is that the New Testament writers were perfectly willing to borrow familiar ideas, just as preachers today quote from movies or the comics or the lyrics of popular songs to make their point.

We find other practical moral advice in what are often called "Household Codes." These are instructions to members of the Christian family. The most complete example is in Colossians 3:12–4:1, which gives advice in three pairs: to wives and husbands, children and fathers, and slaves and masters. Ephesians 5:21–6:9 is based directly on this passage. One reason for suspecting that Paul did not write either of these letters is that all other references to these codes are found in later New Testament writings. None of them includes all three pairs, but they do add a new dimension: Christians should respect worldly rulers (advice missing in Revelation!). These passages are 1 Peter 2:13–3:7; 1 Timothy 2:1–15; 6:1–2; and Titus 2:2–3:2. Romans 13:1–7, where Paul urges Christians to be subject to the governing authorities, may draw upon one of these codes. The key commands are "be subject," "submit," "obey." The codes reflect the desire for a stable social order, in the same way that the teachings of Confucius do in another culture.

What do they really say about the role of women? On the one hand, they grant women more respect than most Hellenistic and Jewish documents of the period; husbands should love their wives. On the other hand, they express a trend toward the subordination of women in the early church, linked to the growing Christian legal tradition we mentioned earlier.

Supporting Arguments in Early
Christian Wisdom

The early Christians, then, used more than one wisdom tradition to tell us *what* to do (its content). But do they give us any reasons *why* we should lead a moral life?

The arguments in James are similar to the ones we saw in Proverbs. Wisdom is one of God's gifts to those who ask (1:5); it is "from above" (3:17) and not "earthly, unspiritual, devilish" (3:15). We should want it because it is "pure, then peaceable, gentle, willing to yield, full of mercy and good fruits" and because it brings a "harvest of righteousness" (3:17–18). Thus wisdom is a means to the good life that James has described. For James, both wisdom and law help us to understand the life-style or ethos of the Christian community.

Paul makes the same basic point when he uses the list of vices and virtues in Galatians. Vices are earthly and unspiritual. Virtues come easily to us when we are open to God's spirit. These virtues are not rules we have to follow but examples of the way we will live when we "belong to Christ Jesus" (5:24). For Colossians, also, the virtues belong to the new life we have in Christ; they reflect our new life-style or ethos.

Finally, there is nothing unique in the household codes, but they are given a Christian interpretation: "as is fitting in the Lord," "fearing the Lord," "serving the Lord," "knowing that you have a Master in heaven," "out of reverence to Christ," "as to Christ," "for the Lord's sake," and so on. Ephesians develops the image of the church as the bride of Christ as a kind of commentary on the relationship of wives and husbands.

Authority
in New Testament Wisdom

James claims no special authority for his message, in contrast to the New Testament prophets and to John's visions. Neither does he claim to be a trained interpreter of Scripture. He writes in order to shape the moral character of one or more local Christian communities. Those communities should not be oriented toward the world but should be more concerned to maintain their own identity.

We do not find any appeal to divine revelation in any of the passages we have examined. Instead, wisdom is simple, practical advice about the best way to live. In these cases, the New Testament writers are borrowing and baptizing the best moral insights of the world around them. Why should we be afraid to do the same thing?

Exercise 23

1. *In the first exercise in this chapter, you listed people and/or writings that gave you "wisdom." Do you want to change that list or add anything to it?*
2. *Do you agree that there are important sources of moral insight outside the Christian faith? If so, what are some of them?*

6

The Moral Life According to the Bible

So far, we have discovered four different ways of thinking about the moral life, all of them found in the Bible. The *legal* approach is based on a body of revealed rules, commandments, or moral codes. These develop into a written tradition and so have a fairly fixed form. This requires a class of persons (priests, scribes, bishops) to interpret them for the community. Ethicists refer to this as a "divine command" approach to moral thinking. A second approach is the *prophetic*. The prophets are often aware of the legal tradition and appeal to it, but their primary claim to authority is a new and direct revelation of God's purpose through word or vision. In calling people to be faithful to God, the message is shaped by the circumstances of the prophet and those who hear his or her words. The *apocalyptic* approach is similar to the prophetic, since it appeals to direct revelation. However, it differs from prophecy in the extent to which it uses exotic symbols, focuses on the future, and reinforces the purity of the community. Finally, *wisdom* appeals not to revelation but to rational insights into moral behavior. Most of these insights are not limited to the covenant community but are shared with other cultures of the time.

We need to admit that the four styles are almost never found in a pure form. The Torah reflects prophetic concerns for justice, just as the prophets quote from the Law. Both the wisdom literature and the apocalyptic book of Daniel refer to the Torah, in very different ways. For James, the Law and wisdom are almost identical, while Paul views Christ as the Wisdom of God who sets aside the Torah as a basis for our salvation. If we had time, we might look at the way in which each biblical writer combines two or more styles of moral reflection.

The next obvious question is "So what?" Are all four patterns equally valid? How are they supposed to help us as we wrestle with moral questions in our own lives?

Exercise 24

Your local congregation owns a house next door to the church. It is now vacant, and the church has been asked to convert it to a temporary shelter for battered women and their children. Many neighbors are opposed to the idea because it may bring "undesirables" into the neighborhood and drive down property values. You serve on the governing body of your congregation, which will meet in a few days to decide the issue. You want to open the meeting by saying something about "the biblical view" on this issue. What will you say?

MORALITY IN A BIBLICAL PERSPECTIVE

First, you might say that *the Bible does not answer all of our questions.* This may be hard to accept, especially if you have been taught to believe that the Bible is a book that has all the answers. Next to the stove in our kitchen is a little pamphlet that tells how to deal with emergencies like removing stains or getting rid of odors. Lots of times we treat the Bible like that pamphlet, as a place we can go to find the answer to whatever problem is bothering us. For example, the edition of the New International Version that I have includes, as do some other editions of the Bible, hints at the end on "Finding God's Answers to Personal Problems." It lists some typical problems that we face (such as insecurity, loneliness, temptation, and guilt) and for each gives two or three passages from Scripture. Significantly, there is no mention of social issues. Now, there is nothing wrong with going to the Bible for guidance. We do not do it often enough. However, if we expect to find one or two verses that will tell us what to do about providing a shelter for battered women or housing for the homeless or food for the hungry, we have missed the point of what the Bible is saying to us about the moral life.

You might also remind your friends that *there are several biblical views*. If the Bible was written by real human beings who lived in real communities, and if they had the same kind of freedom that we do, we should not expect them to agree any more than people do today, even in church! On a specific topic such as divorce, for example, biblical writers do speak against it, but not always with the same advice, and not always for the same reasons. In the case of spouse and child abuse, the Bible has almost nothing to say directly.

You could point out the four styles of moral reflection that we have studied and point out that *diversity is a gift*. How poor we would be if we had only one Gospel portrait of Jesus. Having four Gospels (and many others outside the canon) creates a much greater richness, like having a kaleidoscope that gives us new patterns as we turn it. How poor we would be if the Bible contained only law or only apocalyptic. We should celebrate the fact that we do not have only one way of thinking about the moral life, but several rich patterns.

You could add that *all four styles belong in the Bible*, so we need to listen to all of them. This goes back to the question of biblical authority, which we discussed in the opening chapter. If we do not listen to the variety of approaches, then we will inevitably pick out those passages or that style (for example, the prophetic) which fits our own way of thinking. Then we can claim that our own view is the "biblical" one.

Finally, you could show how *the Bible helps to shape our moral perspective*. A careful reading of the Bible helps to develop our sensitivity to moral issues. Each of the four biblical styles can help us to develop a sense of responsibility, as I will show in the final chapter.

Put differently, you could argue that the Bible teaches us *how to decide, not what to decide*. The Bible teaches us that we need to wrestle with these issues in the community of faith. Each of the four styles we have studied includes important arguments about *why* we should be moral and *how* we should respond to what God has done, is doing, and will do. Therefore, you might ask your colleagues how each style might look at spouse abuse. Both the Torah and the prophets emphasize the need to care for widows and orphans. Jesus and Paul and the New Testament prophets redefine "family" to mean the community of faith. The wisdom tradition models self-control in the family setting, and the Household Codes encourage husbands to love and respect their wives, not to subdue them. In other words, you should not look for one or two texts that will tell you what to say. Instead, look for what the Bible has to say about what it means to be a family, and what happens to those who do not have a family to support them. When the Bible talks about the value of suffering, is it talking about innocent victims within a family? What does it say about people who inflict suffering on others?[1] In exercise 24, then, the real issue is not "What will the neighbors think?" but "Who is my neighbor?" Is there a real need for a shelter? If so, what is the church's responsibility to meet that need?

These are only suggestions to show how the Bible can help us to address difficult issues. In this section, we have been concerned with questions of *style*. The way the Bible shapes our perspective or our way of looking at moral issues and not the content of specific passages is the heart of a "biblical morality." However, the Bible also teaches us how to be the church, how to create a new ethos. Let us try to find out what that means.

BIBLICAL "ETHICS" OR BIBLICAL "ETHOS"?

"Ethics," as we saw in chapter 1, is the task of spelling out general principles of moral behavior, while "morality" is the task of applying those principles to specific situations such as the one described in exercise 24. "Ethos," by contrast, refers to the customs or the life-style of a particular group of people. Every group has generally accepted ways of behaving. Often these are taken for granted; they may not need to be written or even spoken. The ethos of a yacht club, for instance, is quite different from that of a bowling league. Almost without exception, the biblical writers are primarily more interested in shaping the ethos of their hearers and readers than in talking about moral principles.

In this section, then, we will focus more on the *content* of biblical morality, which is its *vision of human community*. In each of the four styles, we have seen how the biblical writers spell out different dimensions of such a vision. If you have time, you may want to go back to those earlier chapters and see where we have talked about that vision. Otherwise, we will look briefly at three examples, all drawn from the New Testament.

The real thrust of Paul's "gospel" is to help his churches develop a new ethos, a new pattern of conduct. Time and again he gives moral advice. He tells the Thessalonians not to be idle while they wait for the Parousia. He tells the Corinthians what to do about a case of incest, and then answers their questions about sex, marriage, and other topics. In the lists of virtues and vices, he gives us models of what we should do and not do. When he gives these specific instructions, however, he rarely lays down a new law for us to follow. He is giving us examples of a new life-style. In effect, he is saying, "This is how you ought to live as a Christian."

Paul's gospel begins with the claim that Christ's death and resurrection have bridged the gap between God and human sinners. To dramatize that claim, he uses several metaphors drawn from the social life of his time. *Redemption* is an economic image, based on the fee that purchases a slave's freedom. *Justification* is a legal image, picturing a judge who pronounces a verdict of "not guilty." *Reconciliation* is a familiar image of restoring broken human relationships and overcoming alienation. He also uses the image of *the body of Christ* to show

how we can participate in the Spirit and the life of the risen Christ. Have these images and metaphors lost their power today? Are there others that would make the same point in a more vivid way?

Paul also shows no interest in "ethics" in our modern sense. He does not draw out abstract principles that we can then apply to every problem that we face. For him, the moral life means living out our new relationship to God. Think of the many ways in which Paul tries to make that point. He says that we should shape our lives in response to God's call. He tells us that we are set apart for God, using terms like "holy" and "saints" and "sanctified." Our lives should reflect our faith and our hope and especially our love. We should treat our bodies as members of the body of Christ. Since we are in the Spirit, or the Spirit in us, our lives should show the fruits of that presence. We ought to imitate Paul, just as he imitates Christ, at least in his willingness to suffer for the sake of the gospel. We are to be transformed and renewed rather than to conform to the standards of this world. All of this is Paul's language.

As we read Paul, he is asking what this new life in Christ means for us today. Even though our situation is vastly different from the ones in Corinth or Galatia or Thessalonica, Paul's gospel asks us to choose and to act responsibly. Even though we may disagree with other Christians about abortion or affirmative action or sending American troops into conflict overseas, the church is the place where we must work out the shape of the Christian life. If we are free in Christ, we must dare to open our lives to constant renewal by God's Spirit. If we are members of the Body of Christ, we are never completely alone in our decision making. We need to share those difficult choices with others in the community of faith. Working out that ethos is our answer to the question "Why read the Bible, anyway?"

Similarly, we cannot really call James an ethicist in our modern sense. Rather, he is a teacher of moral wisdom. The purpose of his teaching is to shape the moral character of a community, which originally may have been more than one group in one location. If we belong to such a community, as James sees it, we should govern ourselves by "the law of love" and by the wisdom "from above" that God gives. We should distinguish ourselves from the rest of the world by our love for one another, by our care for widows and orphans, by visiting the sick, by regular prayer, and above all by self-discipline. When he attacks the rich who oppress, and when he promises that worldly poverty will be reversed at "the coming of the Lord," James is creating a sense of group identity and moral integrity. If we took James's advice literally, we would become what many commentators have called a community of the "pious poor." If we are not prepared to do that, then we must answer the question "What is distinctive about our life as a Christian community?"

John of Patmos is just as eager to shape the ethos of the churches to which he sends his letters and his visions. He uses the burning threat of martyrdom to forge them into people made of steel. Resist the temptations of a secular culture, he tells them, even if it means that you will be persecuted. We find almost no specific moral advice in Revelation, of the kind we see in the legal and wisdom traditions. Rather, John calls us to be faithful in everything we do to the sovereign God and to the crucified/triumphant Christ. In a recent book, Ward Ewing interprets Revelation as a "theology of liberation" for middle-class Americans who feel trapped by powers outside their control.[2] Although his argument does not always work, it reminds us that the message of the Apocalypse is not only for the poor and persecuted. Even though we do not face the same problems as the churches of Asia Minor, John asks us how our churches are distinct from other social organizations.

Exercise 25

If you have time, you may want to answer or discuss the following questions.

1. *Do you agree that we should focus not just on what the Bible says but on how it helps us to make moral choices? Why or why not?*

2. *Do you agree that Christians ought to have a different life-style from non-Christians? If so, what are some of the characteristics of that ethos? If you are feeling creative, you might pretend that you are a modern Paul or James and write a letter to a church in your community.*

THE RELEVANCE OF A BIBLICAL ETHOS

How can the contemporary church remain faithful to the biblical vision? During most of its first three hundred years, the church remained a minority group within the Roman Empire. Christians could try to maintain the New Testament pattern of church life, since the conditions had not changed that much. When the church was granted legal standing and Christians gained positions of power and influence, the conditions changed radically. Add to that the amazing changes in technology, especially within the past one hundred years. Then add new ways of thinking, like the deep-rooted individualism that has been part of our culture since the Enlightenment. These three changes—in context, in technology, and in ideas—are not the only ones we could mention, but by themselves they underline the distance we have to move when we try to relate the Bible to moral decisions facing us.

The main thrust of the Bible is its vision of human community, its concern with shaping the ethos of a community faithful to God. More than anything else, this means that the church must be *a community of moral discourse*. The church is the place where moral issues ought to be discussed and debated. At the risk of badly oversimplifying, let me suggest that there are two general models for relating the biblical ethos to the church in our time.

One model is *the church speaking to itself*. The first step in this process is *listening to Scripture*. Studying the Bible is the first step in knowing what it means to be a community of faith and a moral community. In the work of Stanley Hauerwas and others, "narrative" or "story" is the way to do ethics. The church is a "Community of Character." The church is a "story-formed community"; it shapes the character of its members by telling and retelling its story.[3] This is certainly an essential part of what the church does.

A second step in the church talking to itself is *listening to tradition*. The Bible is only the beginning of a moral tradition that continues to grow. The Torah began as an oral tradition, gradually passed into a fixed written form, and then produced groups of interpreters whose job was to apply the Torah to new situations. In a similar way, the early church began to develop its own tradition of moral advice and moral instruction. That process has never stopped.

Protestants tend to treat the formation of a "canon" or collection of Scripture as an act of God rather than a product of church use over a long period. Before the last book of the Bible was written, however, several other Christian writers were giving moral advice, and we need to listen to what they said. By the time our New Testament was generally accepted (at the end of the fourth Christian century), there was already a long list of Christian leaders explaining how to understand it. When we say that the Bible is the beginning of a moral tradition, then, we mean that we have to listen to other voices in the early church. Also, we have to see how other Christian thinkers like Augustine and Aquinas and Luther and Calvin have interpreted passages from Scripture. Even those churches that claim to embody the New Testament pattern have their own tradition of interpreting Scripture that goes back to their founders in the Reformation period or later.

The third step in this conversation within the church is *deciding what it means to be distinctive*. If nothing else, the biblical ethos means that the people of God (Israel, the church) must show the rest of the world how God wants them to live. In the words of the Mennonite scholar John Howard Yoder, "The church is called to be now what the world is called to be ultimately."[4]

For many churches this has meant trying to restore or recreate the ethos of the early church. What exactly does that mean? Does it mean rejecting practices not explicitly mentioned in the New Testament like the Primitive Baptists, who do not have Sunday schools, and the Churches of Christ, who do not use musical instruments? Does it mean a different pattern of dress, like many Amish and Mennonites and Old Order German Baptists ("Dunkards")? Does it mean a strict separation of the sexes, like the Shakers? To be like the New Testament churches, in a literal sense, we would have to adopt their social and economic patterns. To become churches like the ones James and John of Patmos were addressing, we would have to give up most of our possessions and become sectarian communities. We would have to reject most modern culture, including its technology.

Being a Christian ought to make a difference in the way we live. Our life-style ought to be distinctive in some way. What makes the church different from Rotary or the PTA or Alcoholics Anonymous? The church, as a community of moral discourse, is the place where we should be talking about that.

The other model is *the church talking with the world*. This is a two-way conversation. On the one hand, it means *listening to the challenges* with which the world confronts us. For example, members of our congregations are increasingly faced with moral questions about the use of organ transplants, about genetically determining the sex of a child, about surrogate parenting, and about terminating life or extending it mechanically. Developments in contraception, sterilization, and abortion techniques have accounted in large part for the sexual revolution in our society. The availability of drugs and handguns has created an atmosphere of violence in many of our cities. The problem of providing food and shelter for the homeless is still with us.

Many Christians feel that we have no business discussing these challenges in church. We should make our personal decisions about how to respond, or the government should deal with them. During an adult class that was discussing one of Scott Peck's books about relating psychology and religion, a member of the class said that she had told her neighbor what we were studying. "Well," said the neighbor, "you have no business talking about that in church. You shouldn't be studying anything except the Bible." There, clearly expressed, is the difference between the two models.

The other side of the conversation is *sharing with the world the biblical vision of human society*. There are various ways of doing this, some of which we will examine in the next chapter. One approach to sharing the biblical vision is found in the work of John Howard Yoder and Stanley Hauerwas, whom I cited earlier in this chapter. They believe that the biblical story— particularly the story of Jesus Christ—gives us the model for a nonviolent social ethic. By incorporating that story, church members model for the rest of the world what God intends for human community.

During the spring term of 1990, I directed a Washington Semester program for a consortium of five Lutheran Colleges, now under the auspices of The Luther Institute. One important part of our program was to look at what churches are doing in the nation's capital to deal with the need for housing and food and health care for those who cannot afford it. The Church of the Savior and Luther Place Church and many others have developed creative, effective ways of dealing with these issues as churches. These same problems exist in virtually every community, especially in a time of business decline. Like these, our churches can learn to develop a distinctive ethos by becoming sensitive to human needs in the church, in the local community, and in the larger world. Then we can also discuss in the church how to respond to those needs as a community. That is a large part of what the Bible has to say about the moral life.

Exercise 26

1. *In the previous exercise, you were asked to think about what should characterize a Christian life-style. Do you want to change your view now that you have read the last part of this chapter?*
2. *Do you prefer the model of the church talking to itself or the church talking to the world? Why?*

PART TWO

THE BIBLE
AND CHURCH
SOCIAL POLICY

7

Churches and Social Policy

In this chapter we will turn our attention away from the Bible itself. Instead, we will begin to look at "the use of the Bible in Christian ethics," as we called it in chapter 1. To be more specific, we will ask how church bodies have used Scripture to develop or to support their position on social issues.

Exercise 27

Before you read this chapter, take time to answer these questions. If you are part of a class or study group, you will probably want to discuss your answers with one another.

1. *Does the Christian faith guide you as an individual to make decisions about social issues such as capital punishment or gun control or smoking in public places? If so, how? If not, why not?*
2. *Should the church, through its leadership, tell you what position you should take on those or similar issues? Why or why not?*
3. *Should the church, through its leadership, try to influence the*

*positions legislators and other public officials take on these
and similar issues? Why or why not?*

Before looking at what the churches have actually said, we will
begin by looking at four possible "models" or patterns that
churches have used to deal with social and political issues. As I
will show, these four models are simply a different way of
packaging what we called in the last chapter "the church
speaking to itself" and "the church talking with the world."
Once we have looked at them, then we will ask how social
policy statements function in different religious bodies. We
need to do this if we want to know who is speaking, and with
what kind of authority, and to whom. We will also take a very
general look at the way in which these statements use biblical
and theological insights.

HOW CHURCHES DEAL
WITH SOCIAL ISSUES

Robert Benne has written a helpful article entitled "The Church
and Politics: Four Possible Connections." He identifies four different ways in which the churches have traditionally dealt with
these issues (see table 7.1).[1]

TABLE 7.1
Benne's Four Models for Church and Politics

	Unintentional	*Intentional*
Indirect	1. The Ethics of Character	2. The Ethics of Conscience
Direct		3. The Church as Social Conscience
		4. The Church with Power

In table 7.1 "indirect" means that a church body, as an institution, does not try to become involved in public life or to influence social policy. In contrast, a "direct" approach uses the church's resources (such as publicity and staff) to bring about social change. The "intentional" versus "unintentional" distinction hinges on whether or not the church has a clear vision of the type of social change it wants to bring about.

The first model, *the ethics of character*, refers to that type of church which focuses on the personal formation of its members through liturgy, teaching, and church discipline. It does not expect its members to be active in public affairs, and it makes no effort to take a stand on social and political issues. James and the letters of John and the Apocalypse represent that model in the New Testament. Today, this is the model we called in the last chapter "the church talking to itself." The focus is almost completely on the spiritual development of its members. The goal is to protect the identity of the community and to be a witness to the world but not to transform society.

A much more popular model on the American scene is the second one, *ethics of conscience*. Put simply, this approach focuses on "consciousness raising." It is intentional in the sense of trying to make people more aware of social issues. At the same time, it does not try to tell individual Christians what position they should take or what they should do about those issues. Thus it is indirect, leaving the decision to the individual conscience. This model is the church "listening to the challenges" of the world.

The third model is the one that will concern us for the next two chapters. In Benne's words, " 'direct' in this third type means that the church becomes a public actor as an institution in addition to its indirect effects through its laity."[2] It seeks, deliberately and intentionally, to influence the shape of the larger society. The most popular way of trying to do this, at least in the last thirty years, has been through social pronouncements. These statements not only inform legislators and other public officials where the church body stands on a particular issue but also guide the moral reflection of church people.

We need to be clear, however, that the term *"influence"* is the key to this third model. It is only through persuasion, through the use of arguments, that the church tries to push forward its vision of a just society. This, and also the next model, are examples of the church "sharing with the world the biblical vision of human society."

The fourth model is also direct and intentional, since it involves the church as an institutional actor. However, according to this model, the church makes use of its *power* to threaten or coerce a particular line of action. Benne uses the examples of community organization activities that are supported by church funds, or the support the Polish church gave to the Solidarity movement. He includes "advocacy" in this category, that is, the work of church people in supporting the church's pronouncements. Whether this is the use of power, as distinct from influence, is a point that needs more discussion.

THE ROLE OF CHURCH
SOCIAL POLICY STATEMENTS

Most of the major Protestant denominations have an office or agency that is responsible for developing position statements on social issues. The process differs, but it almost always includes clergy and laypersons who are experts on the particular issue, and there are usually one or more hearings to get a broader involvement of church members. Most of the denominations also have an office in Washington, D.C., to represent the churches' interests where public policy is being shaped and implemented. In some cases, the churches even maintain offices in state capitals.

In 1990 I examined most of the statements that had been issued up to that time by the American Baptist Churches, the Evangelical Lutheran Church in America, the United Methodist Church, the Presbyterian Church (U.S.A.), and the United Church of Christ. Also, to give a broader spectrum, I considered statements by the National Association of Evangelicals (an umbrella organization for roughly fifteen million evangelical

Christians in the United States) and the National Conference of Catholic Bishops. Both the Lutherans and the Presbyterians have merged or reunited since 1980, so I included statements from the earlier bodies as well.[3] In this chapter I will try to present a general idea of what is in these statements. In the next two chapters, we will look at a few representative statements, which I will summarize in more detail. In the appendix I have listed addresses for each of these church bodies, so that you can write for individual copies or request other information.

Types of Statements and Their Authority

When we read these statements, we need to be aware of who the *audience* is. Many of them are addressed to members of that denomination, to educate them and motivate them to act. In these statements, the church is speaking to itself or is listening to the challenges of the world. Other statements are addressed, either primarily or secondarily, to policymakers in the public sphere. They represent the church speaking to the world. Very often, a statement is simply vague on this point.

We also need to know what *status* a statement has. Most denominations distinguish at least two types: those that are advisory in nature and those that set policy for the church body. Basically these relate to the two types of audiences we noted above (church members and policymakers). In addition to official statements, churches often publish background papers and study documents, but we will not consider them here.

The American Baptist Churches distinguish broad policy statements from specific resolutions, which must actually cite one or more policy statements on which they depend. Both of these require the approval of the General Board of the denomination. The Evangelical Lutheran Church in America makes a similar distinction between broad social teaching statements, directed primarily to the church, and social practice statements applying the social teaching to specific issues. The United Methodist Church has had a statement entitled "Social Principles" since 1972, which has been revised periodically. These principles identify social issues in six areas: the natural world, the nurturing community, the social community, the economic community, the political community, and the world community. Resolutions are usually more specific and are grouped under the same headings as the social principles. These may contain several pages of recommendations for action. The Presbyterian Church (U.S.A.) makes a similar distinction between a social policy statement and a resolution. Within the United Church of Christ, as a covenant church, each agency is relatively autonomous. In practice, this means that each national agency can develop its own statements, and each biennial General Synod speaks only for itself. However, most of the agencies refer to a General Synod statement, when it exists, since it is more representative of the denomination as a whole.

The National Association of Evangelicals focuses on informing individual Christians about social issues, so it adopts resolutions only on issues where there is a high degree of consensus among its members. Nevertheless, since 1956 about two hundred resolutions have been adopted by the annual conventions, often more than one on the same issue.

Finally, we need to determine the *authority* of each statement and its recommendations. Often the church bodies include a disclaimer as well as a claim. For example, "American Baptists have also recognized that Christians studying the Scripture can come to differing views concerning the meaning of that scripture for their individual lives and for society. . . . In such discussions, respect for persons who hold differing views is essential."[4] Lutherans consistently recognize the ambiguity of moral choices. In particular, they recognize that there is not just one biblical point of view, nor is there just one public policy position that we can draw from the Bible. For example: "Scripture provides a clear orientation for what God requires of human life, but it does not by itself tell us what we should do in each situation. The diversity of responses to God in Scripture make it ill suited to be a neat moral code."[5] For United Methodists, the Social Principles "are intended to be instructive and persuasive in the best prophetic spirit" and are meant to "call to all members of The United Methodist Church to a prayerful, studied dialogue of faith and practice."[6] For Presbyterians, as for the Lutherans, social statements do not have the same authority as confessions. A task force study document went out of its way to insist that "General Assembly social policy statements are persuasive and advisory (not coercive and binding) in their authority for synods, presbyteries, sessions, and church members, encouraging their contextual witness."[7] The United Church of Christ statements are not binding on local congregations or individuals, but "all UCC members are expected to take these statements seriously and to consider if God is speaking to them through the statements of these various bodies."[8]

All statements of the National Association of Evangelicals, in the words of a 1963 resolution, assume "the Scriptures of the Old and New Testament to be the sole authority for the believer and the church and the only infallible rule of faith and practice."[9] This does not claim authority for the statements themselves, but it does point to a more fixed foundation than appears in the other positions we have just examined.

Statements by the National Conference of Catholic Bishops, of course, depend on a long tradition of Roman Catholic social teaching that includes papal encyclicals and documents issued by Vatican II. Nevertheless, in the "Peace Pastoral" that we will examine later, the bishops went out of their way to distinguish "universally binding moral principles found in the teaching of the Church" from their own policy recommendations and applications. "However, we expect Catholics to give our moral judgments serious consideration when they are forming their own views on specific problems."[10]

THE USE OF SCRIPTURE: GENERAL COMMENTS

Before we look at what the churches have said about peace issues and abortion, we can make some general comments about the use of Scripture in social policy statements.

Prominent themes in the American Baptist statements are

human freedom, particularly religious liberty, and church-state relations. No effort is made to derive these completely from the Bible, since "Church and State in the modern sense were unknown in biblical Israel."[11] Most of the Baptist policy statements contain an extensive biblical and theological basis for their position. This is not always true of the resolutions, because they depend on the policy statements.

Most of the Lutheran statements contain a strong biblical-theological emphasis. Usually they do not appeal to particular biblical passages, but instead they focus on broad themes such as creation, sin, justification, the body of Christ, and new life in the Spirit. This is especially true in the excellent study document *The Church in Society*, which was prepared as a foundation for all future social statements. A traditional Lutheran emphasis on the "two kingdoms" (the church and the world) is used consistently in this document to inform the church's position on social issues.

The United Methodist social principles also draw out broad biblical and theological motifs, but in a very condensed form. A consistent emphasis in these principles and in many of the resolutions is the worth of the individual, which is supported by an appeal to human rights. A small number of the resolutions (about twenty) include an important biblical-theological discussion. About half of them have no biblical or theological references. In some cases this is because the resolution deals with a very practical issue, or because the church's position is already clear. Typically, we find examples of what we discussed in chapter 1: citing one or two verses out of context (proof texting) or appealing to biblical "principles" such as love, justice, *shalom* (peace), responsible parenthood, and privacy without giving them any specific content. Most of these resolutions are sophisticated in their use of social scientific data. However, unless they are just as sophisticated in their use of Scripture and tradition, they will not provide much help in shaping the church's ethos.

The position of the Presbyterian churches is formed not just by Scripture but by the confessions of the Reformed tradition.

That tradition, like the Lutheran, has emphasized the proper role of civil authority, which may include the use of force to maintain order. However, the Reformed tradition has also placed a greater emphasis on the role of individual conscience, which may include rebellion against unjust authority; and it has emphasized the importance of transforming the social order to be more obedient to God's purpose for humanity. Those emphases are reflected in many of the social pronouncements. Presbyterians require six components in all social policy reports and statements of the General Assembly. The first of these is "biblical-theological reflection consistent with Reformed faith."[12] Unfortunately, that is not always done in much detail, including the Task Force report that includes this statement. Most statements, however, are more careful and more thorough in the way they use Scripture.

The United Church of Christ statements almost always include a section on their biblical, theological, and ethical background. Most often they emphasize the prophetic style at the expense of the others; they fail to maintain a balance between the prophetic and pastoral emphases. At other times, the biblical perspective is not really integrated into the recommendations, or the biblical passages cited do not really support the theological conclusions. Sometimes, only one or two passages are cited.

Most of the resolutions of the National Association of Evangelicals do not actually explain their biblical or theological rationale. That is unfortunate, because it would be helpful to know whether these statements are appealing to different texts, or whether they are giving the same texts a different interpretation.

SOME CRITERIA FOR THE USE OF SCRIPTURE

I have already suggested that some statements are better than others in the way they use Scripture. In fact, if we ask, "What is an appropriate way to use the Bible in a social policy statement?" there are several criteria we can use. I modestly call these the "Sleeper rules" for a good statement:

1. It does not take all of its quotations from one of the four patterns of moral reflection (for example, the law or the prophets), but it selects biblical citations from a variety of sources.
2. It avoids proof texting, that is, taking one or more verses out of their original context and applying them directly to a contemporary issue.
3. It avoids appealing to broad ethical themes in the Bible, such as "peace" or "justice," unless it gives them some specific content.
4. It shows how the biblical material (usually part of a broader theological statement) relates to the policy recommendations.

Exercise 28

1. *Do you agree with these criteria? Are there others that you would like to add to the list?*
2. *Do you agree that the main purpose of these statements should be to shape the ethos of the church? Why or why not? How could that be done more effectively?*

8

Issues That Divide: Nuclear Weapons

During the 1980s, more and more Americans became convinced that we were facing nuclear annihilation. As the tensions of the Cold War increased, many people were concerned about the survival of the human race. Our foreign policy was based on nuclear deterrence, or "mutually assured destruction." In this view, if both the United States and the Soviet Union had equivalent stockpiles of nuclear weapons, neither would initiate an attack, knowing that their own country's major cities and military targets would be struck in retaliation. This view was parodied in the movie *Dr. Strangelove*. In 1983 ABC aired *The Day After*, a made-for-TV movie showing the effect of a nuclear attack on Kansas City. The cover story of *Newsweek* for November 21 of that year was a look at the psychic fallout of "TV's Nuclear Nightmare." Popular writers often referred to the "balance of terror," to the effects of a "nuclear winter," and to "psychic numbing." In addition, a lively and sometimes bitter public policy debate focused on President Reagan's proposal to develop the Strategic Defense Initiative, popularly known as "Star Wars."

Fear of this nuclear holocaust spawned a variety of protests. Books such as Jonathan Schell's *The Fate of the Earth* helped to focus public attention. In it, he argued, "The question now before the human species, therefore, is whether life or death will prevail on earth. This is not metaphorical language but a literal description of the present state of affairs."[1] Protest movements such as SANE, Another Mother for Peace, and Fellowship of Reconciliation became increasingly active. Many young people were sure there would be a nuclear war within their lifetimes. A sixteen-year-old girl appearing before a House committee said, "I think about the bomb just about every day now. It makes me feel sad and depressed when I think about a bomb being dropped. I hope I'm with my family. I don't want to die alone."[2]

Many church bodies felt the situation was so critical that they had to say something, either to their own members or to policymakers or to both. In this chapter, we will look at some of their responses. Our interest is primarily in the way in which the churches used Scripture in their statements. We will look first at the most pertinent biblical passages, then at traditional Christian positions on issues of war and peace, and finally at some examples of recent church policy statements.

With the thaw in the Cold War, you may be wondering why we should still be interested in such statements. First, they are excellent examples of the way in which churches have spoken about urgent public issues. Second, questions of the control of nuclear weapons and disarmament remain critical. The problem of nuclear proliferation and the possibility of nuclear terrorism may become even more serious in years to come. Finally, many of the same moral issues arise with the use of chemical or biological weapons, a threat that became real during the Persian Gulf crisis.

Exercise 29

Before we move ahead, try to remember how you felt during the situation in the early and middle eighties.

1. *Did you feel that nuclear weapons were essential to our na-*

tional security, or were you afraid that they were a threat to
world peace?

2. Did you feel that the churches ought to take a stand on the use
   of nuclear weapons? If so, what did you think they should say?

BIBLICAL ATTITUDES TOWARD WAR
AND PEACE

The biblical writers, of course, know nothing about nuclear
weapons, so they cannot give us any direct guidance about
their use. The texts themselves do not give us a moral position
on such a complicated issue. Also, as we have seen, the biblical
writers do not all speak with the same voice; there are a variety
of perspectives on moral issues. What we have to look for, then,
are broader clues about biblical views of war and peace.

If we look again at *the Law* as an approach to the moral life,
we discover an interesting tension between the Old and New
Testaments. In the Torah, warfare is clearly acceptable as an
instrument of foreign policy, as it is today in the modern state
of Israel. Indeed, the book of Deuteronomy promotes the idea
of a "holy war," not only against Israel's foreign enemies but
also against deviant forms of religion. Such words are put into
the mouth of Moses by the Deuteronomic writers in the latter
half of the seventh century B.C.E., and they became a platform
for King Josiah's social and religious reforms. The "holy war"
involves taking no prisoners but killing them instead. The Israelites are not to intermarry with the Canaanite inhabitants of the
land; they are rather to destroy the Canaanite shrines and religious objects (Deuteronomy 7:1–6, among other similar passages). Deuteronomy 20 contains more specific regulations for
the conduct of war. Basic to this view is the notion of *herem*, or
what is "devoted to God" in a cultic or ritual pledge. The spoils
of war belong to God; therefore, they must be destroyed rather
than used for personal gain. The Deuteronomic editors of Israel's history (the books of Joshua through Kings) read this
view back into the story of Israel's conquest of Canaan and into
the story of the monarchy. Clear examples are Joshua's destruc-

tion of the cities of Jericho and Ai (Joshua 6:21; 8:20–29), Saul's defeat of the Amalekites (1 Samuel 15), and Elijah's slaughter of the prophets of Baal (1 Kings 18:40). We simply do not know to what extent this view of the holy war was actually carried out, but the picture of God as a warrior, as a "jealous god" fighting for Israel's sovereignty, was widely shared. This idea of a holy war, later adopted by Islam, is ruthless because it treats the opponents as the enemies of God.

On the other hand, the commandment "You shall not kill" (the New English Bible and the New International Version translate it as "murder") has often been interpreted as an absolute command of God and as a basis for Christian pacifism. However, from what we have just seen, there was no general prohibition against war in the Torah and Exodus 21 gives a number of legal precedents for capital punishment.

When we turn to the New Testament, the context changes dramatically. The "new covenant" no longer refers to Israel's struggle for a national and religious identity. Instead, it refers to communities of people who believe that Jesus has revealed God's will. In a variety of ways, New Testament writers try to explain how the church can include Gentiles and at the same time be the legitimate heir to God's promises to Israel. National identity is out of the picture, since these communities—tiny by our modern standards—must survive under Roman domination.

As we have seen, a persistent theme in the New Testament writings is the "love commandment" or the "law of love." Actually, this appears in three different forms. In the Gospel and letters of John, as we saw in chapter 2, "love" applies to other Christians. "Love one another" is an appeal to resolve conflicts within the Johannine community. In other passages that cite the verse "Love your neighbor as yourself," such as Romans 13:9 and James 2:8, the circle is widened to include non-Christians as well as those within the church. The most dramatic form of Jesus' saying is found in the Sermon on the Mount in the charge to "Love your enemies" (Matthew 5:44), even in the face of persecution. The love command, then, represents a "new law" only in the general sense of a moral norm or moral principle. "The pacifism of the early church was derived not from a New Testament legalism, but from an effort to apply what was taken to be the mind of Christ."[3]

Granted that love is a central theme in the New Testament, the next question is how to interpret it. First, it is always a *relational* or *social* term. It applies to our relationship to God and to other persons; it is never used in the modern sense of an attitude or an emotion, like "falling in love." Second, it is *a norm*, in the sense of telling us *how* to deal with others. At the very least, it applies to conduct within the Christian community, but most New Testament writers also see it as a norm for Christians as they relate to people outside the church. Third, it is *not a social program*, in the sense of a blueprint for Roman society. That society was ruled by a fairly small and elite group; the early Christians were not in any position to influence them. Nevertheless, in the long run the church's ethos did have a transforming effect on the larger society.

In some Christian writers of the second and third centuries, the phrase "the law of Christ" was used to support Christian pacifism. Unfortunately, the New Testament writers do not connect love that directly to issues of war and peace. Later, the Catholic tradition came to treat love as a norm for those within the religious orders, but not as a requirement for ordinary Christians. It represents a more exclusive kind of devotion. Another pattern, especially in the Lutheran tradition, claims love as a norm for personal relationships but does not see how it can function in more complex social structures (the "orders of creation"). In any of these cases, there is a long step from treating love as a norm for the Christian life to making it the basis of national policy.

Exercise 30

1. *Does the idea of a "holy war" have any place in a Christian morality? Why or why not?*
2. *Does "the law of love" or "the law of Christ" give us as Chris-*

tians a sufficient basis for dealing with issues of war and peace? Why or why not?

The *prophetic* perspective is also somewhat ambiguous. As we have seen, one theme of the Old Testament prophets concerned Israel's response to foreign domination. During the years when the Northern Kingdom was threatened by Syria and Assyria, Isaiah of Jerusalem consistently advised the kings of Judah not to make alliances with any foreign powers. When Judah was under attack by its neighbors to the north, Isaiah gave King Ahaz a sign in the famous "Immanuel" passage. A woman will conceive, and "before the child knows how to refuse the evil and choose the good, the land before whose two kings you are in dread will be deserted" (Isaiah 7:16). Later, during a siege of Jerusalem, Isaiah advised King Hezekiah not to surrender. God had promised to preserve David's line. Based on this "royal theology," Isaiah was confident that God would save the city; and in fact Sennacherib and his troops did withdraw, suddenly and mysteriously, and return home (Isaiah 36–37). The phrase that best summarizes his view is "in returning and rest you shall be saved, in quietness and trust shall be your strength" (30:15). While not a pacifist in our modern sense, Isaiah insisted that confidence in God was more important than buying protection from a larger, more powerful nation. Over one hundred years later, Jeremiah gave virtually the opposite advice. Facing an attack by the Babylonians, Jeremiah urged the king to surrender rather than fight a long, bloody battle in which Jerusalem would be devastated (Jeremiah 6, 21, 27). For him, the destruction of the city would be God's punishment for Israel's unfaithfulness. God's judgment is worked out by using other nations. What these prophets shared was the view that trust in God means more than relying on military weapons.

One other theme that emerges in the prophets is the vision of a world at peace. In Isaiah of Jerusalem, this takes the form of a restored Davidic monarchy. The passage in Isaiah 9:1–7, made familiar in Handel's oratorio *The Messiah*, reaches its climax with the claim that "there shall be endless peace for the throne of David and his kingdom. He will establish it and uphold it with justice and with righteousness from this time onward and forevermore." It is basically a nationalistic vision, and it will take place on this earth, not in some celestial realm. It will be a time of peace (*shalom* in Hebrew). Note that this peace is not just an absence of conflict; it is a positive rule of justice. "The effect of righteousness will be peace, and the result of righteousness, quietness and trust forever" (Isaiah 32:17). Similar sentiments are expressed by Jeremiah (for example, 33:15–16). Ezekiel promises an everlasting covenant of peace (37:26). Isaiah 40–55, those marvelous poems written in the spirit of Isaiah during the Exile, promise a restored nation and much more. The other nations, drawn by Israel's suffering, will come to worship her God, and nature itself will be renewed (see 51:7–11; 55:1–13). This vision of peace is primarily theological; that is, it depends on the action of God to set things right. It is also focused on the future (eschatological), so it is not a blueprint to tell us how to act on social issues.

When we turn to the New Testament, we immediately have to realize that many of the people who met Jesus thought of him in prophetic rather than messianic terms. In the tradition of the Old Testament prophets, he called people into a new relationship with God based on love and not on strict ritual purity. He called people to acknowledge the lordship or rule of God in every aspect of their lives. More than that, he began to create a community of followers who would practice a new ethos, a new life-style based on love for other human beings. His life, and also his death, modeled the kind of sacrificial love that should also be reflected in the lives of those who "follow" him. John Howard Yoder has argued that Jesus self-consciously put forward a "social ethic" that rejected economic exploitation and violent conflict as a way of life.[4] Specifically, Jesus rejected the Zealot option of an armed revolt against Roman domination. Many details of Yoder's argument have been challenged by Richard Horsley, who has shown that Zealots as a party did not exist until the Jewish War, a generation after Jesus.[5] Horsley does agree, however, that Jesus was a social revolutionary, and he argues that Jesus actually escalated conflicts with his opponents. Certainly, Jesus was a threat to the authority of the Jewish leaders, and Pilate was convinced that Jesus was enough of a troublemaker that he should be executed.

Jesus formed a community whose ethos was radically different from that of other Jewish groups, and of course different from Hellenistic patterns as well. His style was not "political," as we understand that term. Instead, he released the power to civilize, to transform people into a community under God's rule. The early church kept that revolutionary power alive by redefining "family" not as blood relatives but as other believers. The church took over the language of the household.[6] Paul also tapped that power to create an inclusive community in which "there is no longer Jew or Greek, there is no longer slave or free, there is no longer male and female; for all of you are one in Christ Jesus" (Galatians 3:28).

Actually we know very little about Jesus' attitude toward war. His saying "Render to Caesar what is Caesar's" acknowledges the authority of Rome to tax, but it says nothing about its police powers. Jesus did not prevent his disciples from carrying swords, but at his arrest he condemned their use. The cleansing of the Temple was a prophetic act of protest. The Beatitude "Blessed are the peacemakers" really has a more apocalyptic thrust, since they will receive their reward in the Kingdom of Heaven. Whatever questions we may have about the authenticity of some of Jesus' sayings, the Gospels show us a Jesus who exemplified and taught a nonviolent life-style. The difficult question is how we can translate that into the life of the church today, and even more how we can relate it to issues of public policy.

The *apocalyptic* tradition does not introduce many new themes, but it does extend some that we have already noticed. In the first place, military images dramatize the final conflict between good and evil, which apocalyptic writers expect to happen in the near future. In chapter 4, we have already looked at some of those, so you may want to review those pages. The faithful may have to suffer at the hands of their enemies, but the enemies in turn will be conquered, and those who endure persecution will be rewarded with everlasting life. How much of this conflict is real and how much is metaphorical? The sufferings or "tribulations" facing the faithful are (or are expected to be) real. We must assume, therefore, that people who read and heard these apocalyptic writings really expected God to punish their enemies in some visible way.[7] However, the point to keep in mind is that believers are not urged to retaliate but to endure.

In some New Testament writers, we find the motif that Christ has already defeated or disarmed the powers of evil, so it is only a matter of time before that victory becomes apparent on the world scene. We find the classic expression of this motif in Colossians 2:15, which points to the cross as the event in which Christ's victory was won.

Closely related to this is the theme of reconciliation. Christ's death has not only reconciled sinners to God. It has also healed social divisions, particularly between Jews and Gentiles (for example, Ephesians 2). Ultimately, this reconciliation will lead to the kind of peace that the prophets anticipated. Although this apocalyptic theme does not speak directly to the question of warfare, it does provide a broader theological context that is used, as we shall see, in several church statements.

The *wisdom* tradition does not speak directly to the issue of warfare, either. As we have seen, it deals primarily with individual decision and with interpersonal relationships. It warns against quarreling and sees desire or greed as the source of most conflicts. Proverbs reinforces the need for rulers to act with righteousness (20:28) and to follow wise guidance in the conduct of war (20:18). Ecclesiastes takes it for granted that there is a time for war and a time for peace (3:8). The general impression, then, is that war is a fact of life.

Although it has no direct advice to give us, this style of thinking does become important in the later Christian tradition. It opens the way to critical thinking about the conditions of a "just" war. Rather than ask, "What does God say about war?"

this approach asks, "As rational human beings, under what conditions should we agree to go to war, and how should we conduct it?" To understand this position, we need to look more closely at the views of war that have developed in the Christian tradition.

Exercise 31

Based on these passages, and others that you may want to add, write out your own answer: How does the Bible inform your vision of the human community? What does that vision imply about the place and/or use of nuclear weapons?

CHRISTIAN ATTITUDES TOWARD WAR

Christian pacifism, as far as we can tell from the sources that we have, was the position of the church until the time of Constantine at the beginning of the fourth century, when the church gained official recognition. During that early period, Christians refused to participate in war. Gradually, Christians did serve in the Roman army, which also functioned as a police force.

The Protestant Reformation put its emphasis on "Scripture alone" as the source of authority. In an effort to reconstruct the ethos of the New Testament period, several "peace churches" emerged during the sixteenth and seventeenth centuries. Some of them, such as the followers of Jacob Hutter and Menno Simons, were persecuted by both Catholics and Protestants. They differed in the degree to which they were willing to take part in politics, but all of them shared minority status. The best known of those peace churches today are the Brethren, the Mennonites, and the Quakers.

As the name implies, the pacifist position is a refusal to participate in war. In the past forty years, churches not part of that tradition have gradually come to accept conscientious objection, to war in general or even to particular wars, as a legitimate position. There are still many gray areas, such as serving in the armed forces in a noncombatant capacity or working for a defense contractor. Also, there is a difference between those who equate pacifism with nonresistance as a life-style and others who use nonviolence simply as a strategy for social change.

During the Middle Ages, the church developed a view of war that is generally rejected today: the *crusade*. Drawing on the "holy war" concept of the Old Testament, the crusades became a way to show religious devotion by crushing the infidels. Later, "the Reformed Churches moved in the direction of the crusade, partly because they became involved in wars of religion and partly because of their theocratic concept of the Church."[8]

Even though most churches no longer endorse the crusade as a strategy for waging war, there is still a tendency on the part of some Christians to see war as a conflict between good (our side) and evil (the opponents). When President Reagan characterized the Soviet Union as "the evil empire," he was giving voice to a secular version of the holy war theory.

The moral failure of this view has been described well by Joseph Allen: "The dominant feature is the sense of moral self-righteousness and moral indignation toward supposed wrong-doers. The sense of compassion is lacking. . . . Crusaders lose the awareness of their own sin as well as of the continued worth of the wrong-doer."[9]

The predominant Christian way of viewing war has been the *just war* theory. As we have noted, it did not originate in the Bible. Instead, it entered the Christian tradition from Hellenistic sources, particularly Stoic philosophy. Augustine and, later, Thomas Aquinas gave the theory a Christian orientation. There is a vast literature on this topic, some of which is listed in the bibliography of this book. Since virtually all the church policy statements we shall consider recognize this position, even if they do not endorse it, we should look at it briefly. Perhaps the best way to do so is by looking at one of the statements, *In Defense of Creation*, by the United Methodist Council of Bishops. It makes the traditional distinction between criteria for resorting to war (*jus ad bellum*) and those for the conduct of war (*jus in bello*):

The five most common *jus ad bellum* principles are:

(1) *Just cause.* A decision for war must vindicate justice itself in response to some serious evil, such as an aggressive attack.

(2) *Just intent.* The ends sought in a decision for war must include the restoration of peace with justice and must not seek self-aggrandizement or the total devastation of another nation.

(3) *Last resort.* This tradition shares with pacifism a moral presumption against going to war—but is prepared to make exceptions. Every possibility of peaceful settlement of a conflict must be tried before war is begun.

(4) *Legitimate authority.* A decision for war may be made and declared only by properly constituted governmental authority.

(5) *Reasonable hope of success.* A decision for war must be based on a prudent expectation that the ends sought can be achieved. It is hardly an act of justice to plunge one's people into the suffering and sacrifice of a suicidal conflict.

The two main *jus in bello* principles are:

(6) *Discrimination.* Justice in the actual conduct of war requires respect for the rights of enemy peoples, especially for the immunity of noncombatants from direct attack. Such respect also rules out atrocities, reprisals, looting, and wanton violence.

(7) *Proportionality.* The amount of damage inflicted must be strictly proportionate to the ends sought. Small-scale injuries should not be avenged by massive suffering, death, and devastation. The war's harm must not exceed the war's good. (Proportionality is also a criterion to be applied to *jus ad bellum*—the decision whether to resort to war in the first place.)[10]

We can easily see, then, that the Bible alone has not been the only criterion in shaping Christian thinking about war, and even when it has served as a source, it has been interpreted in quite different ways.

Exercise 32

1. *Which of the three traditional attitudes toward war do you find most congenial? Why?*

2. *Which of the three views do you think is most consistent with the Bible? Why?*

HOW CHURCHES HAVE USED THE BIBLE

If you remember, we began our study by asking the question "Why do church bodies, each claiming to take Scripture as an authority, reach such different conclusions about the moral life?" In chapters 1, 6, and 7 we saw that churches have different assumptions about biblical authority, about ways of interpreting Scripture, and about its use in moral reflection. In chapters 2 through 6, we also looked at diversity within Scripture itself. Now we need to look more specifically at what the churches have said about the use of nuclear weapons. Without going into the details of their positions, we want to discover how the Bible entered into the moral reasoning they used in reaching their conclusions. In other words, how did these churches make the move from the Bible to contemporary social issues?

Church policy statements become outdated very quickly if they speak only to immediate crises or analyze specific weapons systems. Also, new statements frequently appear to replace or supplement old ones. We will try, therefore, to look only at ones that continue to provide policy direction for the various denominations. We will look at them more or less in the order in which they were adopted. In addition to statements from church offices listed in the appendix, other collections or excerpts are available.[11]

The Presbyterians

Although Presbyterians do not stand in the tradition of the peace churches, the denomination did make peacemaking a priority for the 1980s and beyond. The United Presbyterian Church in 1980 and the Presbyterian Church in the United States in 1981 adopted the report "Peacemaking: The Believer's Calling." In 1983, at the first General Assembly of the reunited body, the Presbyterian Church (U.S.A.), they immediately reaffirmed these statements as the basis for its policy. Since then, over half of the local congregations have agreed to carry out some kind of peacemaking effort to implement this program.

In the background section of this report, after an analysis of the nature of the global crisis, the section entitled "Theological and Ethical Bases for Peacemaking" draws on a number of the biblical themes that we have noted: love for the neighbor flowing from the love of God; service to Christ as Lord who is the Prince of Peace; *shalom* as "total well-being, wholeness, fulfillment, health, joyous harmony; God's reconciliation in Jesus Christ." Biblical passages are cited from the various forms of literature, but the dominant perspective is the prophetic. The apocalyptic dimension is muted, so that the pursuit of peace tends to become a political agenda. The task involves risks and courage "because we live in a fallen world where the pursuit of justice for the sake of true peace has many enemies."

Therefore, the next section considers "Theological and Ethical Bases for Policymaking." Over against the prevailing values of our culture—national interest, national security, and power—Christians should work for justice, freedom, and compassionate order. The "Call to Peacemaking" and the specific recommendations of the report, which are the policy sections, focus primarily on what Christians need to do to be peacemakers. In addition to its internal life, the church must speak to the world: *"The Church bears witness to Christ when it nourishes the moral life of the nation for the sake of peace in our world."*

A second major policy statement was developed in response to specific requests ("overtures"), presented to the denomination in the years 1983–1987, for guidance on such issues as the relevance of just war criteria, the practice of nonviolence, tax resistance, and nuclear deterrence. The result, a report adopted by the national governing body (the General Assembly) in 1988, was a deliberate effort to define "Christian Obedience in a Nuclear Age." The rationale is quite different from that of the earlier statement. The opening section, "The Shape of Christian Obedience," affirms "a long-standing tradition of Christian obedience in response to the loving action of God," but the only Scriptural basis offered is the double requirement to love God and neighbor and "the biblical vision of justice and peace." Thus it fails to satisfy "Sleeper rules" 2 and 3. After a lengthy analysis of our current situation, the document concludes: "It is precisely on the basis of the just war doctrine that participation in nuclear war must be condemned" and alternatives must be sought. How does that relate to the biblical-theological rationale of the earlier document? The only other rationale offered in 1988 is in a section on "Just Peace," referring to *shalom*, to "God's special concern for the poor and the powerless," and to "the great biblical visions of global peace." We are reminded, "Such a peace is ultimately God's gift; we need to avoid the proud illusion that we can create it by human effort alone." The rest of the document is a creative set of strategies for "the transformation of the social order." It does not endorse unilateral nuclear disarmament. It views nuclear deterrence as unjust as a permanent means of national defense and calls for a change in national policy. In addition, it calls for further study of a "civilian based national defense" based on nonviolent resistance. Such a study was later carried out, but it basically called on the government to take a position that church members themselves would not support.

What can we conclude from this brief look at the Presbyterian position? First, the basic foundation is the biblical vision of peace, spelled out in a way that is consistent with a pacifist tradition. This needs to be spelled out in more detail, in relation to other biblical emphases such as the holy war. Also, the connection between that vision and just war thinking needs to be spelled out. Second, the primary focus is on the ethos of the Christian community, on what it takes to be peacemakers. The function of these statements is to educate and instruct Christians about their commitment to peace, although some recommendations (for example, the rejection of nuclear war and nuclear deterrence) were to be sent to the president and Congress as well. Finally, "the transformation of the social order" is an important theme:

> The Reformed tradition has given particular emphasis to the calling of Christians to seek such transformation. While we take the power of evil seriously and do not expect transformation to be easy, total, or permanent, we have confidence that the cre-

ative, redeeming, and transforming power of God is at work in human society as well as in the church.[12]

The Roman Catholics

The Challenge to Peace, issued by the U.S. Conference of Catholic bishops in 1983, was a remarkable document in many ways.[13] One was the open process by which the Pastoral was developed. Another was that it was addressed not only to the Catholic community but also to those in public life concerned with "the dangers and dilemmas of the nuclear age." In arriving at its conclusions, the Pastoral has a long section on war and peace in the biblical sources, and it weaves together insights from both the pacifist and just war traditions, calling for a "theology of peace." Finally, among its important conclusions is that a strategy of directing nuclear weapons at population centers (even in retaliation) cannot be justified; neither can a nation that is the first to use such weapons. While recognizing the duty of citizens to support their country in defense against aggression, the bishops make it clear that conscientious objection is a legitimate option if it includes alternative service.

The Pastoral begins with an introduction that identifies the reason for the letter as "a moment of crisis," the threat of nuclear war to the existence of our planet. Part I, "Peace in the Modern World: Religious Perspectives and Principles," deals with Scripture in the context of traditional Catholic social teaching; we will return to this part for a closer look. In part II, "War and Peace in the Modern World: Problems and Principles," the bishops address directly the morality of nuclear weapons. They recognize that the potential destruction of the planet in a nuclear war creates an unprecedented situation ("a new moment"). Those aspects of nuclear war mentioned above (targeting noncombatants, first strike) are morally unjustified, according to traditional just war principles. A number of policy choices are discussed in this section and in part III, "The Promotion of Peace: Proposals and Policies." Part IV is a collection of specific advice for Catholics under the heading "The Pastoral Challenge and Response." The letter ends with a brief concluding section.

The biblical section is treated within part I under the heading of "Peace and the Kingdom." It begins with three important comments about the proper method for interpreting Scripture. First, the term "peace" is used in many different ways, so we must note the context. Second, the biblical writings reflect historical situations that are quite different from our own. Third, "Since the Scriptures speak primarily of God's intervention in history, they contain no specific treatise on war and peace." Within the Old Testament, we find the image of God as warrior, although this image is gradually transformed. Peace is seen as a gift from God but is viewed primarily in terms of the covenant people rather than of individual well-being. Particularly in the writings of the prophets, there arose the vision of God's eventual reign of righteousness and peace (*shalom*).

Turning to the New Testament, the letter examines military images, Jesus' message of "God's reign as one in which love is an active, life-giving, inclusive force," and finally "Jesus and the community of believers." Through the experience of Jesus' love and his gift of the spirit, Christians formed a community marked by a ministry of reconciliation and by a discipleship reaching out to the whole world. The next section in the Pastoral, "Kingdom and History," is a reminder that, as Christians, we cannot expect the Kingdom of God within history as a result of our own effort. The biblical vision of peace does not lead to a perfectionist ethic.

We need to note several things about this treatment of Scripture. First, even though it tends to focus primarily on the vision of individual prophets and on the Gospels, it does meet our criteria for an adequate statement. Second, it admits that the Bible alone cannot provide answers to complex policy issues:

> Even a brief examination of war and peace in the scriptures makes it clear that they do not provide us with detailed answers to the specifics of the questions which we face today. . . . The sacred texts do, however, provide us with urgent direction when we look at today's concrete realities. The fullness of eschatological peace remains before us in hope and yet the gift of peace is

already ours in the reconciliation effected in Jesus Christ. (paragraph 55)

Third, a key issue is how well this biblical perspective informs the conclusions of the document. Charles Curran notes that the bishops do not appeal to Scripture as the basis for either general principles or policy recommendations. Rather, he says, the Pastoral uses Scripture to give us a vision of the values of peace and justice, so it helps us to understand what it means to be a responsible Christian.[14] In chapter 10 I will argue that this is the right way to use Scripture in Christian ethics.

National Association of Evangelicals

In 1986 the National Association of Evangelicals adopted *"Guidelines" for Peace, Freedom and Security Studies*.[15] This is not actually a social pronouncement but rather the design of an ambitious program. Thus it describes program objectives, criteria for assessing their success, and administrative arrangements for carrying out the program.

The primary goal of this program is to spell out an Evangelical position that will avoid the extremes of "Peace and Disarmament" and "Security and Liberty." In other words, the goal is to develop a mediating position. On the one hand, it will affirm the need for resolving international conflicts nonviolently. On the other, it will also affirm the values of a strong military posture, of religious liberty, and of democracy. In order to carry out this program, the priorities are to develop (1) a core of leadership within the Evangelical churches and their agencies, (2) a resource center of information and speakers, and (3) media coverage. It is essentially an educational program.

The *Guidelines* reflect the attitude toward Scripture that we noted in the last chapter: "A commitment to Biblical authority is a fundamental reference point for Evangelicals affiliated with the NAE." One section of the *Guidelines* is entitled "Biblical Foundations." It acknowledges sin and redemption as basic theological categories. More important, it draws from the Bible six "principles" that should guide Christian action in society:

1. The church's task is primarily spiritual, although this "does not preclude Christian activity in political matters."
2. Christians are "called to serve the world." This means intimate involvement with other human beings; it involves social responsibility.
3. Christians bear witness to God's reconciling work.
4. At the same time, Christians are called to a ministry of reconciliation, of peacemaking.
5. "Biblical realism" means that we should not expect perfection or world peace through our own efforts.
6. That point is reinforced by "Biblical visions of the future." However these apocalyptic visions are understood, they remind us, "We cannot create the Kingdom of God; we can nurture a human future congruent with the Kingdom's values."

The actual biblical passages cited in this section are drawn primarily from the sayings of Jesus, from Paul's letters, and from various prophets. The perspective is broad enough so that it does not violate the "Sleeper rules."

In fact, several of the "Assessment Criteria" reinforce points we have already made about the use of Scripture:

3. Do our programs acknowledge the full range of Biblical perspectives on war, peace, security and freedom?
4. Do we understand that the Kingdom of God is a matter of God's time, not our own? Have we defined responsible, morally sound ways to bring considerations of that vision into our work in the hard soil of this world's realities?
5. Have we defined "peace," "justice," and the relationship between them in ways that take account of both the eschatological meaning of Shalom and our historical responsibilities and opportunities this side of the coming of the Kingdom in its fulness? (p. 32)

An important paragraph (p. 21) also deals with the danger of treating the Bible as a simple set of solutions to contemporary problems. It warns against using the Bible to support positions arrived at on other grounds.

Drawing inferences from Scripture is a delicate and fallible exercise. Every effort must be made to understand the legitimate and rational grounds for opposing viewpoints. . . . The Evangelical commitment to the authority of Scripture necessitates a willingness to take the entire Bible seriously. (p. 21)

On the surface, there is little difference between this use of the Bible and the point of view we have seen in the statements of other denominations. Yet these *Guidelines* are a conscious alternative to the positions taken by many of those denominations. How can we account for the differences? Is the greater emphasis on religious liberty and national security derived directly from the Bible, or does it reflect the dominant values of our own culture? How is the greater emphasis on military strength related to apocalyptic, the view that "the Kingdom of God is a matter of God's time, not our own"? Is that emphasis more closely related to the "holy war" and "crusade" views? These are some of the questions that need to be explored.

Other Denominational Statements

Other denominations also issued statements, which we cannot examine in as much detail here. The Lutheran Church in America adopted one entitled "Peace and Politics" in 1984, calling on church members to commit themselves to "the politics of peace." Biblical passages are incorporated into broad theological affirmations. In line with the Lutheran view of the "two kingdoms," there is a provocative section "The Creator's Presence in the Political Work of Peace." In 1985 the American Baptists approved "Policy Statement on Peace," which will serve for a long time as the foundation for future resolutions. "Biblical/Theological Basis" is a long and excellent section in that document developing "the visible witness of the church as a growing, caring community."

Within the United Church of Christ, peace has long been a major item on the agenda. In 1981 the denomination resolved to become a "Peace Church," and in 1985 this process was completed with the adoption of a pronouncement "Affirming the United Church of Christ as a Just Peace Church." The rationale is very brief, so that the biblical basis is not really developed. The key perspective, almost a slogan, is that of a "just peace." We have already quoted from *In Defense of Creation*, issued by the United Methodist bishops in 1986. The statement is extremely detailed in its treatment of various weapons systems, but it is also the only one of the Methodist statements with an extended rationale. The biblical section develops the theme of *shalom* as "the sum total of moral and spiritual qualities in a community whose life is in harmony with God's creation" (p. 26). In the Old Testament, *shalom* embraces the themes of creation, covenant, and community. In the New Testament, it is treated under the heading "Jesus Christ Is Our Peace": "Ultimately, New Testament faith is a message of hope about God's plan and purpose for human destiny" (p. 28).

SUMMARY

What can we conclude, then, about the use of Scripture in these policy statements? First, these longer policy statements—in contrast to shorter statements and resolutions—satisfy the "Sleeper rules," though in greater or lesser degrees. Out of the available biblical passages, we can see a tendency to draw on the themes of peace, justice, reconciliation. Statements by the American Baptists, the Catholic bishops, and the Methodist bishops do the best job of dealing with violence and the holy war; several of the other statements simply ignore that dimension of the biblical texts.

Second, although we have not looked at their conclusions in much detail, there are broad areas of agreement. All agree there is a Christian *presumption against war*, even when it is not stated in those terms. From a Christian perspective, war is not a desirable way for countries or other groups to deal with each other. Also, all agree that nuclear war is unacceptable. Usually that conclusion is based on a just war argument, although some seem to derive that conclusion more directly from the biblical vision.

Third, there are areas of disagreement. The Catholic bishops reluctantly accept the necessity of nuclear deterrence as an interim step toward disarmament. Some of the other statements dismiss deterrence as immoral or unjust. Also, the issue of national security is treated differently. The sharpest contrast would be between the statements by the Presbyterians (calling for study of a nonviolent, civilian-based defense) and the United Church of Christ, on the one hand, and the National Association of Evangelicals, on the other.

Thus the same Bible is used in different ways to arrive, in some cases, at different conclusions.

Exercise 33

1. *Which impresses you more, the amount of agreement or the amount of disagreement in the way these church bodies used Scripture to deal with the use of nuclear weapons?*
2. *A friend of mine has a bumper sticker that reads "God hates war." Do you agree or disagree? How do you know?*

9

Issues That Divide: Abortion

Although many churches have long been concerned about abortion as an aspect of sexual morality, only in the 1960s did they begin to speak about it as a matter of public policy. The *Roe v. Wade* decision by the Supreme Court in 1973 focused attention on the policy aspects of the issue. Contrary to much popular opinion, the Court did not legalize "abortion on demand." It did permit abortions within the first trimester of pregnancy with the consent of the physician, but after that point, it recognized that the government has an interest in protecting the life of the unborn fetus. Since that decision, debate on the abortion issue has become increasingly polarized. Roman Catholic and conservative Protestant groups officially support a "pro-life" position, while the mainline Protestant denominations are deeply divided even if they have taken a position.[1] The Court's 1989 decision *Webster v. Reproductive Health Services* had the effect of returning this debate to state legislatures. Each new appointment to the Supreme Court increases the likelihood that the 1973 decision will be severely modified if not overturned. Thus the abortion debate will continue in the 1990s. It is our equivalent of the prohibition debates of the 1920s.

Exercise 34

A Task Force is currently working to define your denomination's position on abortion. Your congregation has been asked to give the Task Force three pieces of information: what you think that position should be, what Scripture passages support that position, and what other arguments support your view. As a member of the governing body of your congregation (remember exercise 24), draft your answer to those three questions so that you can take it to a meeting next week. You may want to share your answers with others in your group and see if you can reach a consensus.

WHAT ARE THE ISSUES?

The public debate about abortion seems to have set the agenda for the churches. It is an example of "the church listening to the world." Most of the church statements deal with these issues, implicitly if not explicitly. Although the biblical perspective does not provide us with clear-cut answers to the world's agenda, it may help us to frame the agenda in more positive ways. First, let us look at four key issues in the public policy debate.

When does "life" begin? Is it at the moment of conception? Is it at the point, coinciding roughly with the end of the first trimester, when movement by the fetus can be detected (often called "quickening" or "hominization")? Is it when the fetus is "viable" and could survive outside the womb? Or is it at birth? All of these positions have been argued on biblical and other religious grounds. In the contemporary debate, the real issue is whether or not to define the fetus as a "person," with legal rights, from the moment of conception. Neither the biological evidence nor theological arguments are clear enough to be convincing to both sides in the debate. Therefore, the answer to this question is more of a basic assumption than a conclusion. For example, a statement by the Assemblies of God asserts that "it is obvious the organism is human and alive before birth. Human life is potential only before the male sperm and female

142

ovum join to form a new living human being."[2] Unfortunately, this assertion is not as "obvious" to everyone.

Who should make the decision whether or not to abort? Is it the expectant mother? If she is a minor, should she have to get permission from one parent or both parents and/or a physician? What role should the physician play, especially at later stages in the pregnancy? What role do legislatures have in protecting the fetus or in preserving the health of the mother? What role should the courts have in this process?

Recent church statements do not address all of these issues directly, but they do touch on them. Most statements adopt a position that is basically "pro-life" or "pro-choice," usually with some qualifications. If they deal with unwanted pregnancies, they usually call for some kind of counseling, but they do not agree whether this should include information about abortion as an option.

What role should the churches play in the public policy debate? Some church statements are primarily advisory; that is, they speak to church members with the aim of shaping their lives. Other statements, on both sides of the issue, want to make the church's position into the law of the land. The disagreement is not just over style but also over substance. The issue is not just how Christians should live but whether the secular society should adopt a Christian ethos. This is an excellent example of issues we talked about in chapters 6 and 7.

If we want the churches to help shape public policy, do we argue strictly on the basis of Christian morality, or do we take into account the "social costs"? On the one hand, we might estimate how much the American economy has lost, in terms of productivity, from the millions of children who would have been born if the mothers had carried them to term. On the other hand, we could also point to the cost of medical care and social services for more children who would have been born into poverty or neglect. Is that a cost the churches would be willing and able to assume, or would it simply add to the public debt? Should these factors even be considered?

Furthermore, how far should the churches carry their involvement? If we are against abortion, should we also oppose federal funding for clinics that give information about abortion, experiments using fetal tissue, and the sale of a "morning after" birth control drug such as RU 486? If we favor the option to abort under certain conditions, should we then provide counseling for women who later regret their decision?

Finally, *under what conditions is abortion acceptable*? Is it permissible when the mother's life is at stake? Is it when she is the victim of rape or incest? Is it when the girl is twelve years old and mentally retarded? Is it when the mother is in her forties, recently divorced, and starting a new job to support two other children? If we belong to churches that speak about "the sanctity of human life" or about the value of God's creation, we will likely have a hard time treating abortion as a means of birth control. Therefore it becomes hard for us to draw a line when we try to make exceptions. Under what conditions do you think abortion should be permitted? Compare your list with the arguments that you used in exercise 34. See if you want to change the position paper you wrote.

WHAT THE CHURCHES HAVE SAID

In this section, we will look at what a variety of churches, including the ones we examined in the last two chapters, have said about abortion. Fortunately, on this issue, there is available an excellent collection of statements from a whole range of church bodies.[3]

Historically, the development of Christian thinking on this issue parallels thinking about war and peace. One source is the New Testament. "The historical source of the Catholic teaching on abortion was the conviction of the early Christian community that abortion is incompatible with and forbidden by the fundamental Christian norm of love, a norm which forbade the taking of life."[4] Early writers do not support their stand on abortion by citing specific biblical passages. Instead, they appeal to love as a moral norm, which should guide Christians in their daily living.

The other source is the idea of natural law. By the time of Augustine at the beginning of the fourth century, abortion—like contraception—was regarded as a moral evil because it frustrated the natural purpose of sexual intercourse, which was defined as procreation. Although later Christian writers, including Aquinas, disagreed on the precise moment when the fetus became "ensouled" and therefore a fully human being, the "conceptus" was at least potentially a unique person. To interfere with its normal development was to go against nature and therefore against the design of God.

Contemporary churches are divided on the abortion issues mentioned above, and on others as well. For example, Roy Enquist studied the statements of seventeen denominations and identified four approaches. Both "prohibitionists" and "qualified prohibitionists" see protecting innocent life as the highest value. "Aretologists" (derived from the Greek term for "virtue") leave room for a variety of values and feel that abortion may be a tragic necessity under certain circumstances. "Individualists" emphasize liberty and resist any restrictions on individual conscience.[5] He does not, however, explore the question that interests us, namely, how the churches use the Bible in arriving at and supporting their moral stance.

A few church statements *cite specific texts to show that abortion violates the commandments of God*. For example, the Presbyterian Church in America bases its absolute prohibition of abortion on the sixth commandment. In answer to the question whether the fetus is a "person" created in God's image, a 1978 statement affirms "While Scripture may not provide a precise scientific statement in answer to this question, the theological understanding of man revealed in Scripture leaves no doubt about the continuity of personhood which includes the unborn child."[6] We will look at some of the relevant texts in the next section.

Most statements *refer to passages which show that God is involved with the creation and life of the fetus*. This is true of denominations as diverse as Assemblies of God, Church of God (Anderson, Ind.), Church of the Brethren, and the Reformed

Church in America. While admitting that Scripture does not explicitly identify the point at which personhood begins, this approach does support the idea of the sanctity of life even in the uterus.

A third approach is *an appeal to broad theological motifs within Scripture*. For example, a 1987 resolution by the American Baptists speaks about "life as a sacred and gracious gift of God." It acknowledges different points of view within the denomination and refuses to adopt a specific public policy position, leaving that decision to individuals. In its *Social Principles*, the United Methodist Church speaks about "the sanctity of unborn life" and recognizes "the sacredness and well-being of the mother." It opposes abortion as a means of birth control or gender selection. It speaks about the tragic possibility of abortion without saying what conditions would justify it.

The Presbyterian Church (U.S.A.) in 1983 approved companion statements on "The Covenant of Life and the Caring Community" and "Covenant and Creation: Theological Reflections on Contraception and Abortion." These would permit abortion in a variety of circumstances, including inadequate financial resources. The theological basis is "the covenantal character of parental responsibility" and a biblical emphasis on "the need for personal moral choice." Both statements contain a number of specific recommendations on technical issues dealing with the origins and termination of life, genetic choices, health care, contraception, and abortion. Theologically, there are only a few general appeals to God as revealer and creator, to the value of human life, and to our responsibility as stewards.

The United Church of Christ has long held a strong position favoring women's rights. The pronouncement "Sexuality and Abortion" by General Synod 16 (1987) tries to ensure that persons facing unplanned pregnancies are informed about all options open to them, including parenting the child and abortion. Except for the comment "Scripture teaches that all human life is precious in God's sight and teaches the importance of personal moral freedom," the statement provides no other biblical

and theological reflection, since it presupposes the pronouncements of earlier General Synods. For the most part, the affirmations in this third approach are too general and so violate
"Sleeper rule" 3.

The most definitive statement of the Roman Catholic
Church's position is found in the encyclical "Humanae Vitae"
by Pope Paul VI. In the Peace Pastoral, the American bishops
equated the loss of innocent life in war with aggression and
violence against the unborn.[7] In response, their position has
come to be called a "consistent ethic" of reverence for life. In
1975, following the *Roe v. Wade* decision, the bishops issued a
"Pastoral Plan for Pro-Life Activities: a Reaffirmation," revising
a plan originally issued ten years earlier. It called for a threefold
program of public information and education, pastoral care,
and public policy. The last part contains specific recommendations for pro-life activities at all levels within the Catholic
Church, including citizens' lobbies within congressional dis-
tricts. The plan assumes that natural law is a clear, convincing
basis for legislation protecting the rights of the unborn. Natural
law also provides a common ground on which Christians and
non-Christians can cooperate.

Although earlier we have not studied the positions of individual ethicists, we should look at the work of two writers who
have tried to change the way in which churches think about
abortion.

Stanley Hauerwas, in an early article, argued that from the
point of view of the moral agent the real question we need to
ask is "What is abortion?" While assuming that "there are
good reasons to consider the *conceptus* as life" and that we
should not make a conscious decision to terminate that life
prematurely, he also recognizes that a woman facing an abortion is personally involved and not a detached spectator.[8] In
other words, the moral question is more subtle than we often
suppose. His later writings on this topic try to shift the focus
away from the liberal presuppositions of our culture to ask,
"How should a Christian regard and care for the fetus as a

child?"[9] The church should aim at developing a distinctive moral consensus, at least among its own members, about conception, childhood, and parenting. The church should focus not on abortion as an isolated decision or action, and not on influencing public policy, but on shaping the character of its membership. Hauerwas's contribution is to insist that the church's ethos should encourage and support childbearing.

From a feminist perspective, Beverly Wildung Harrison argues that women cannot be truly moral agents unless they have the right to make intimate decisions about what happens to their own bodies. If the state preempts that right by making abortion illegal, it in effect says that women are not competent to make moral choices. This point does not mean that women are entitled to "abortion on demand," but it does challenge the idea that women are simply "containers" for fetuses who have an independent, unrelated, and fully human life of their own. She challenges the view that the traditional (Roman Catholic) view was primarily concerned for the life of the fetus. Many Catholic theologians opposed abortion because they associated it with prostitution and adultery; the majority of theologians did not deal with the issue. Similarly, she attacks a deterministic view that the human potential of the fetus is present at the moment of conception. Rather, pregnancy is a system in which the fetus and the mother are interdependent. We can see a tragic example of that when the mother's use of drugs damages the potential of her child. In contrast to Hauerwas, Harrison wants to desacralize the idea of reproduction, and she accepts the cultural definition that abortion represents a conflict of rights between the mother and the fetus. Her contribution is to force us to recognize the role of women as moral agents.

Unfortunately, neither Hauerwas nor Harrison derive their main arguments from Scripture, except in a very indirect way. In his case, the biblical story shapes the church as a "community of character." In her case, "Reproductive choice for women is requisite to any adequate notion of what constitutes a good society."[10]

A BIBLICAL BASIS FOR THINKING
ABOUT ABORTION

In this section, we will look more closely at the way in which the Bible can guide us in our own moral reflection about abortion. The Bible does not answer the public policy questions in a direct way, but it does give us resources for a broader theological and ethical perspective.

The abortion issue *demonstrates clearly the failure of a proof texting approach to Scripture.* The biblical writers simply do not address the issue. Mark Olson has reviewed the texts most often cited in support of a "biblical view" of abortion, and he concludes, "Unfortunately, the Bible offers no direct, overt teaching on the morality or immorality of deliberate, willful abortion. You can search every line of every page from Genesis to Revelation, but you won't find a thing. The subject just isn't dealt with in a direct manner."[11] Like any other "argument from silence," this one leads to different conclusions. Conservative commentators assume that the biblical writers do not mention abortion because they take it for granted that the fetus is a person. More liberal interpreters assume that abortion was permitted, since there is no prohibition against it. Olson is correct that there is no biblical passage that speaks explicitly about abortion, so we need to look at the texts that are most often mentioned.

A key passage is Exodus 21:22–25, which describes the penalty when people are fighting and cause a woman to have a miscarriage. If she loses the baby, her husband gets to dictate the penalty, within limits approved by the judge. If she dies, then the "lex talionis" ("an eye for an eye, a tooth for a tooth") comes into play. In both cases, the woman is essentially treated as his property. Abortion opponents see here a penalty for causing the death of an innocent life,[12] but the lesser penalty for the miscarriage means that the fetus was not treated as a full human being.

Another favorite text for the pro-life position is the commandment "You shall not murder" (Exodus 20:13). Here three questions arise. First, did it originally prohibit all "murder," or only the killing of another Israelite? Second, did it consider the death of a fetus as "murder"? Third, if those who cite this text allow other exceptions to the murder of fully developed human life, in cases such as war or capital punishment, then why not allow some exceptions for a fetus? This text can be used against abortion only if it is part of a consistent ethos of pacifism or nonretaliation.

A third textual argument used by many pro-life advocates is the term *pharmakeia*. It occurs in the list of "vices" in Galatians 5:20 and also in Revelation 9:21 and 21:8. These advocates interpret the term as a ban against chemicals that might induce an abortion. This really strains the meaning of the term in Greek. Virtually all English translations choose terms like "magic" or "sorcery" or "witchcraft."

These arguments are examples of the danger we mentioned in chapter 1 about taking the Bible as a book of moral recipes. The texts do not give us direct answers to the "issues that divide." They do not answer the basic questions we looked at earlier in this chapter. Even if they did speak about abortion, Christian moral reflection demands more of us than simply quoting a few passages from Scripture.

On the other hand, *the Bible does not support the view of the pregnant woman as the "lone decider,"* the only person whose decision matters. Certainly, some biblical writers talk about personal responsibility and about the role of conscience, but that is almost always in a social context, either that of the family or of the community of faith. The Bible simply does not contain anything like our modern notion of individualism, in which we are free to do whatever we please as long as we do not impose on the freedom of others. From a biblical perspective, then, we should never look at the decision whether or not to abort as an isolated act. From our own experience, we know that such a decision almost always involves and affects other people: parents, a husband or lover, other children in the family, in addition to doctors and judges and counselors who may be professionally involved. We need to take those factors much more into account when we talk about this issue.

As we noted, many statements try to develop a broader *biblical view of God's love for all creation.* The announcements to Elizabeth and Mary in Luke 1 show that God is directly involved in generating human life. Several prophetic figures believe that God called them while they were still in the womb (Isaiah 49:1–6; Jeremiah 1:5; Galatians 1:15). Other passages speak of God's "forming" the fetus or a personal identity in the womb (Job 10:8–12; Psalm 51:5; Psalm 139:13–16). All of these passages imply that humans are made in the image of God; they imply the sanctity of human life.

Now, it is important to be clear what these passages do and do not say. Almost all of them describe individuals who have a unique religious consciousness or sense of calling. They do not, therefore, describe a philosophical or legal principle that might help us to decide when truly human life begins or when an abortion is permissible. Like the other texts, they do not answer the questions that we raised at the beginning of this chapter.

What the passages do establish, however, is a *presumption for life.* Even if we do not consider the fetus a "person" from the time of conception, all of the necessary ingredients for human life are present. Barring some action, intentional or otherwise, that terminates its growth, the fetus will develop the potential that is already there. There must be compelling reasons for making a conscious decision to abort. From a biblical perspective, the burden of proof lies with those who make that decision. Abortion as a means of birth control, or as a matter of convenience, does not meet that burden of proof. The primary task of the church should be to develop this ethos among its own members.

At the same time, we have to remember that *the Bible does not glorify biological existence for its own sake.* It is more concerned with what we call the "quality of life." To some extent, this involves a higher standard of living. Poverty and hunger continue to threaten the quality of life for thousands of people every day. The biblical vision of human community may ultimately force us to ask how many people our finite natural resources can support. There is nothing particularly moral about encouraging mothers in Third World countries to bear more children who will later starve to death. Similarly, there is nothing very humane about denying our young people access to birth control information and then also trying to deny them access to safe and legal abortion facilities. Unfortunately, the rhetoric of some pro-life groups suggests that if women can no longer have abortions, they will be deterred from having sex. The experiment with prohibition should have taught us that our appetites cannot be controlled that easily.

Quality of life, from a biblical perspective, is concerned with more than socioeconomic status. It is a search for the meaning of existence, an effort to be faithful to the covenant God. It involves the biblical vision of community. This vision may lead us to find exceptions that will meet the "burden of proof" mentioned above. Pregnancy as a result of rape or incest would fall into this category, but not automatically. Another exception might arise when the birth of a deformed child would mean unmanageable financial and emotional burdens for the family. A decision to abort in such a case would not lie with the mother alone. We would have to consider the kind of support that would be provided by family and friends, the available community health resources, as well as insurance and other financial resources. If the couple are church members, what kind of support, financial and otherwise, is the congregation willing to provide?

The Bible *lends itself more readily to the language of "values" than to that of "rights."* The Bible itself does not use that kind of language. However, the concept of "values" is more consistent with the patterns of biblical reflection on morality, while emphasis on "rights" tends to reflect our modern notions of individualism.

In 1976 the statement "The Value of Human Life" was received by the American Lutheran Church and sent to the

churches as information. It was intended to guide congregations as they wrestle with questions of the environment, economic inequality, and, as one section put it, "Human Control of
Life and Death." In all of these cases, the statement tried to
shift from the language of rights to that of values. "This biblically informed perspective provides that vision of reality which
shapes our understanding of ourselves, our neighbors, and our
world." As focused in Jesus Christ, this means developing a
concern for the neglected. "It also suggests that moral values
such as trust, hope, freedom, and justice must be taken into
account if the purposes of God for human life are not to be
denied."[13] Similarly, a more recent statement adopted by the
1991 Churchwide Assembly of the Evangelical Lutheran
Church in America argues, "Nor is it helpful to use the language of 'rights' in absolute ways that imply no other significant moral claims intrude. A developing life in the womb does
not have an absolute right to be born, nor does a pregnant
woman have an absolute right to terminate a pregnancy."[14]
This is a deliberate effort to move beyond the polarization of
"pro-life" and "pro-choice" to a more moderate position in
the abortion debate. This effort is consistent with a biblical
perspective.

One of the most difficult questions is *the role the churches
should play in the public policy debate* about abortion. That is not
our main concern, but it is worth asking. As we have seen, the
Bible does not give us a "social ethic," at least on the abortion
issue. That is one reason why the Bible has been used in so
many different ways in the debate.

As I have argued, the churches' first task is to shape the ethos
of their own members. Apparently they have not done a particularly good job at this. Recent statistics show that more than a
third of the women polled have a much more liberal view on
this issue than their denominational policy. This suggests that
denominational agencies ought to concentrate more energy on
nurturing their own constituencies.

Even if the churches were successful in doing that job, we
ought to ask whether they should impose that ethos on the

larger society. The churches can and should try to influence the quality of life of the society, but how? One extreme view is that of Gary Potter, speaking as president of Catholics for Political Action.

> When the Christian majority takes over this country there will be no satanic churches, no more free distribution of pornography, no more abortion on demand and no more talk of rights for homosexuals. After the Christian majority takes control, pluralism will be seen as immoral and evil and the state will not permit anybody the right to practice evil.[15]

This is really an attack on the principle of separation of church and state that is guaranteed in the First Amendment to the Constitution.

More disturbing is the stridency and even violence that is used in the name of "Christian love." For example, Frank Morris defends the bombing of abortion clinics by comparing them to the gas chambers in Nazi Germany. He argues that God's moral law justifies violating the civil law of the state, even when it means using violence to eradicate a greater moral evil.[16]

A more promising approach is for Christians to try to find common ground with others. The Roman Catholic appeal to natural law, as we have seen, tries to do precisely that. It insists on the "rights" of the fetus from the time of conception. It bases this claim on biological as well as theological grounds, and in that way tries to find common ground with people whose natural instinct is to treat the fetus as a person. If we want to argue the case in terms of values rather than of rights, then we will have to try to find some other common ground. In the next chapter, I will argue that the notion of responsibility does just that.

A final note is that *the Bible really does help us to grapple with difficult decisions in a more indirect way*. Within the church, it helps to shape our values. It gives us a vision of what human community ought to become. It brings us face to face with God, and so it gives us a new way of seeing ourselves and our world. It helps us to develop a sense of responsibility for our actions.

This position is not always comforting, since it leaves us with the burden of making hard choices, but that is the price we pay for the freedom God has given us.

Exercise 35

1. *Do you agree that the Bible has very little to say in specific terms about abortion? Are there other passages in Scripture that you think should be included in the discussion?*
2. *Do you agree that the language of "values" rather than of "rights" might shift the focus of the abortion debate? If so, how do you think it might lead to different conclusions?*
3. *Look back again at the statement you developed in exercise 34 and see how you might want to change it.*

10

The Bible and Christian Responsibility

Now it is time to draw some threads together. Within the Bible, we have found four different ways of thinking about the moral life. We have also seen how different church bodies have used Scripture when developing social policy statements on complex issues like nuclear weapons and abortion. I feel a little bit like the two spiders in one of my favorite *Far Side* cartoons. They have woven a huge web at the bottom of a playground slide. One spider is saying to the other, "If we pull this off, we'll eat like kings." Well, if we can pull off some general conclusions, perhaps they will nourish us for a while.

ONE BIBLE, MANY INTERPRETATIONS

First, we need to return to the question raised on the first page of this book: Why do church bodies, each claiming to take Scripture as an authority, reach such different conclusions about the moral life? We have already given some answers to that question, but we need to review them, add some others, and then draw out some implications.

First, the Bible was written in a *different historical and cultural context.* Some parts of the Bible, like the laws about farming or sacrifices, simply are not helpful to us because the cultural setting is so different. In other cases, we can use the biblical language only by giving it a new meaning. For example, the Bible talks about God as king, but royalty is not part of the American experience, except in a negative way. When we use that language, then, we have to make an imaginative leap. We are not drawing on an image that is alive in our own experience. That example shows why we must translate or interpret the biblical message as we move from its historical context to our own. When we apply the Bible to the modern world, we should try to do so faithfully, not literally.

Second, in some cases, there are *conflicting viewpoints within the Bible.* The different attitudes toward war found within the Old Testament, and between the Old and New Testaments, provide a clear example of this point. The Old Testament certainly had a more relaxed attitude toward concubines than we find in the early church. First Peter and the pastoral letters see the Roman Empire in a much more positive light than we find in Revelation. The four patterns of moral reflection are not necessarily in conflict with one another, but they often do approach things differently.

Third, in other cases, *the Bible does not deal explicitly with a particular issue.* The obvious case in point is abortion. As we have seen, no biblical text explicitly says that human life begins with conception or explicitly prohibits abortion. The "right to life" position is based on inferences from certain passages (such as Exodus 21:22–25), or on a broader biblical perspective (such as respect for creation), or on sources outside the Bible (for example, the natural law tradition). On the other hand, the view that we make moral decisions as isolated individuals stems more from recent political philosophy than it does from the Bible.

One further reason why churches draw different conclusions about the biblical message is that they are using *different principles of interpretation* and *different theological presuppositions.*[1] We have already noted several instances of this. The differences become much more sharply focused when the debate moves from the church to the public policy arena, as we have seen in the case of abortion policy. Much more ecumenical debate needs to occur at this level, particularly on the status of the Bible as one source of moral wisdom. For example, if Protestant groups appeal to just war principles to some extent in their arguments against nuclear weapons, can they exclude some form of natural law reasoning on the abortion issue? Would it make any difference if the Roman Catholic bishops applied to the abortion issue the same kind of analysis of biblical texts they used in the Peace Pastoral? Evangelicals could also contribute a great deal to such conversations.

One implication of these conclusions is that *the Bible alone does not give us a blueprint for contemporary social policy.* We cannot move directly from biblical texts to recommendations for public policy, a point that several churches noted in the statements reviewed earlier. To make responsible decisions in the public arena, we need to do more than quote biblical passages. We need the information provided by social scientists and by policymakers themselves.

Another implication is that *there is more than one proper way to use the Bible in developing social policy statements,* but some ways are not appropriate. I hope that the four "Sleeper rules" can lead to more thoughtful and more balanced statements in the future.

Finally, we need to remember that *the primary use of Scripture is to help form the ethos or life of the church.* There is no "biblical ethic," as such, but in countless ways the biblical writers try to shape the lives of their readers. To be consistent with this purpose of Scripture, the churches must pay close attention to the role of Scripture in their social statements. The primary use of these statements should be to inform, educate, and motivate church members. If we are not informed, both biblically and theologically, then we have no business making social pronouncements in the name of the church.

A BIBLICAL BASIS FOR CHRISTIAN RESPONSIBILITY

The main contribution of the Bible to Christian ethics is to help us to understand our responsibility as Christians.[2] The Bible teaches us that the faith community is the place where we should learn how to act as the people of God. To say the same thing in a more complex way, the church is the context for responsible action; it shapes what we have called an ethos. The Bible also helps us to see several dimensions of responsible action. It presupposes that God is faithful, and that we also keep faith with others by not lying or betraying them. Next, it takes our freedom for granted as a condition of our action. Christ has set us free from the powers of sin and death; we are responsible for our acts because we have control over them. Third, the Bible focuses on love as the proper norm or standard for everything we do. Finally, it teaches us to act in hope, in the confidence that God will ultimately find what we do worthwhile.

Let us see how each of the four biblical styles can deepen our understanding of our Christian responsibility.

Exercise 36

This exercise is a refresher. Think back to part 1, when we discussed the four approaches to moral reflection in the Bible. What was the most important thing you learned from each? If you can, compare notes with someone else. You may be surprised how different your impressions are.

The Law as a Basis for Moral Life

The *legal* style should be one important part of our own moral life. As the rabbi says in Woody Allen's film *Crimes and Misdemeanors,* "Without the Law, it's all darkness." Because of the way in which New Testament writers thought about the Torah, "law" does not mean that we must obey all of the commandments. It does not mean we should draw up a chart of biblical rules to follow every day, so we can check off the boxes and see how many gold stars we have earned. It does not mean that the Christian life is like scouting, so that we keep earning merit badges until God will have to reward us in the life to come. The problem with so much Christian moral teaching is that it treats God like a cosmic Santa Claus, who brings us presents if we have been good but ignores or even punishes us if we have broken certain rules. We talked about some of these dangers in the last section of chapter 1, when we said that the Bible does not give us moral recipes. Then what does the "law" teach us?

First, it helps us to understand *our need for a tradition*. We have already talked about this at some length in chapter 6. In the Old Testament we see the beginning of a moral tradition as it was interpreted by the priests and then by teachers of the Torah. Later, Jesus and the early Christians reinterpreted that Law, and the leaders of the church began to develop a new legal tradition. In the Roman Catholic and the Orthodox churches, canon (or church) law developed partly as a way of interpreting Scripture and applying it to new situations. The Reformers wanted to bypass creeds and councils and canon law and return directly to the Bible, basing Christian morality on "the Bible alone." In doing that, however, Protestants have developed their own tradition of biblical interpretation. The Bible is now read through the eyes of the Larger Catechism, or the Westminster Confession, or the "fundamentals" and the doctrine of verbal inerrancy. We approach the Bible by some traditional way of understanding it, and that idea of tradition is rooted in the Bible itself. A more contemporary way of making this point is to say that we have a "story," which is not just the story in the Bible but also the way it has been told and retold.

Second, the Law belongs to *the covenant community*. The only reason why the Law exists is to tell us how to live as the people of God. The Law describes the ethos, the behavior, that God expects if we want to be faithful. In the New Testament, this is summarized in the love commandment. Unfortunately, this notion of the covenant community can be applied in quite different ways. On the one hand, there is an *exclusive* interpretation that anyone who violates God's Law must be excluded from the community. This view has a biblical basis in places like 1 Corinthians 5, where Paul tells them to expel the man who is engaging in an incestuous relationship. One church I know expelled a young couple who had recently joined the congregation because they were not attending services regularly enough. Too often during debate over some emotionally charged issue in a church, people on both ends of the spectrum will leave if they do not agree with the position of others within the congregation.

On the other hand, the church can be a place that *tolerates diversity*. It is a place where God's love embraces people who are "at the same time justified and sinners," to use Martin Luther's phrase. Surprisingly, Matthew knew that the church included sinners, in spite of his emphasis on law and righteousness (see Matthew 5:21–24; 13:24–30, 36–50). One Sunday, while attending worship in a new church, I was startled when a member of the congregation asked us to pray for him as he dealt with the symptoms of AIDS. That could not have happened in most congregations I know, so it was obviously a supportive and caring community. Both of these types of community have a "distinctive ethos," but they are quite different. One defines itself in terms of the common identity that the members share. The other defines itself by embracing those who are different.

Exercise 37

1. *Do you think that people listen to what the church says when they have to make difficult choices such as having an abortion, dealing with an abusive spouse, or discovering that a relative has AIDS?*
2. *Should a congregation exclude the people facing those decisions, or should it support them?*
3. *Should the church be a place where these issues are discussed, but people stay together even when they disagree?*

Third, the basis for the law is *the will of God* for human life. The legal tradition points beyond itself to God. The law can never tell us all we need to know about God's purpose, but it can tell us that we owe our lives to the God who created us. Promise keeping is a key to our responsibility as Christians; betraying the trust that others have in us, through lying or deceit, is not.

Prophecy as a Call to Moral Action

The *prophets* point to *God's revelation*. They remind us that God did not stop speaking once the Torah was given. God's will cannot be fully captured in a book, even when that book is the Bible. To be responsible Christians, we need to be open to clues to what God is doing today in events that are shaping our world. Drug addiction and violence in our local communities can be a way in which God calls us to do something. For others, God's claim on our lives comes through hungry and homeless people on our streets. Still others are moved by God's presence in Eastern Europe, in Russia, in the Middle East, in Latin America, and in other countries of the Third World. One of the most important Christian ethicists of the last generation, H. Richard Niebuhr, made this point in a saying that has often been quoted: "Responsibility affirms: 'God is acting in all actions upon you. So respond to all actions upon you as to respond to his action.' "[3]

In particular, the prophets call us to *social responsibility*. What do you think Amos or Isaiah of Jerusalem would say today about the problem of homelessness in our society, or about the pollution of our natural resources? How would they expect us to react? Why? Keep in mind that they did not know our modern distinction between church and state. Does that make a difference in what they might say to us in the church? You may want to look back at the four different models we discussed in chapter 7. The prophetic vision of justice helps us to think about the kind of society we ought to have.

The Apocalyptic Demand
for Religious Purity

The *apocalyptic* style has two traps that we need to avoid. The first is the temptation to make chronological predictions. Whenever apocalyptic interpreters have tied their predictions to a specific timetable, they have lost credibility. Chronological schemes are incidental in most apocalyptic literature, and if we make them the focus we will miss the main point of its message. A second temptation is triumphalism, the tendency to focus on the terrible things that will happen to our enemies, or to gloat because God has promised that we will triumph. This kind of hope is nothing more than a selfish desire for power.

On the other hand, apocalyptic material adds several important insights to our understanding of what it means to be responsible. First, it adds a *sense of urgency*. It prods us to move from reflection to action, to get off our duffs and do something. A Christian lifestyle combines being and doing, thought and action. Apocalyptic reminds us that we may never have another chance to show our love, to share one another's burdens. It teaches us to treasure each moment as though it were our last. In such a situation, Paul told the Thessalonians, "Admonish the idlers, encourage the faint hearted, help the weak, be patient with all of them. See that none of you repays evil for evil, but always seek to do good to one another and to all. Rejoice always, pray without ceasing, give thanks in all circumstances; for this is the will of God in Christ Jesus for you" (1 Thess. 5:14–17).

Second, apocalyptic reminds us that *the church must maintain its identity* in a secular world. The Bible does not tell us exactly how we should do that. However, when we realize what it means to be a Christian, we can never be fully comfortable with injustice and with the forces of evil in the world around us.

Finally, this style *relativizes worldly power*. It teaches us that all social status and all political arrangements are temporary. Is God a Democrat or a Republican? Is God a capitalist or a socialist or a communist? Can any social or economic system survive if it is based purely on human greed and self-interest? On the other hand, is there any economic system that is free from self-interest? According to the apocalyptic point of view, behind all social and economic and political systems stands the one sovereign God. They can survive only if they serve the God "who was, and is, and is to come."

Wisdom as a Guide to Moral Life

The *wisdom* pattern teaches us to be open to sources of moral insight outside the Christian tradition. Down through the history of the church, as Christian thinkers have wrestled with moral issues, they have borrowed insights from philosophers who have struggled with the same issues. In recent years, pastors and counselors have used insights from different forms of therapy. Church administrators have drawn on wisdom from sociologists and management experts. The wisdom literature shows us that it is biblical to use nonbiblical sources! If we are responsible Christians, though, we must test these insights against the authority of the Bible.

Also, more than any other portion of Scripture, the wisdom literature emphasizes the importance of *personal responsibility*. Over and over, the Bible emphasizes the community as the place for shaping moral choices. Wisdom provides an important counterbalance. It appeals to our sense of individualism, even though it emphasizes the important role of parents and teachers. Wisdom means developing self-discipline, self-control, and moderation. (How do you think this message would be received by the teenagers in your church?)

In all of these ways, then, biblical views of morality help us to develop a responsible Christian life-style.

A CHRISTIAN ETHIC
OF RESPONSIBILITY

There are many ways of organizing Christian ethics, but I obviously agree with those who take *responsibility* as the key term.

It is not a biblical term or concept. As Albert Jonsen has pointed out, the earliest use of the term is in the middle of the seventeenth century, so it has not been around for very long, compared to some other moral axioms.[4] However, it does pull together in a remarkable way many insights of the biblical writers.

Even so, there are real obstacles to using this term as a key. The modern mood focuses on the rights of individuals and says very little about personal responsibility. A focus on individuals tends to ignore the idea that we get our values from other people, or that our actions affect others. In a special issue on the American national character, *Time* magazine claimed that we have become a nation of "busybodies" and "crybabies." The busybodies want to impose their morality on everyone else. The crybabies see themselves as "eternal victims"; they blame everyone else for what happens to them and sue for frivolous reasons. Here is just one of the many examples used in that article: "Joel Steinberg, the wife beater and child abuser who was convicted in New York City in 1988 of the battering death of his six-year-old illegally adopted daughter Lisa, told the court, 'I'm a victim, as was everyone else who knew Lisa.' "[5] Others would argue that the national mood is one of hedonism—that is, having a good time, looking for pleasure, enjoying our leisure. Whatever description we may prefer, certainly responsibility is not on the top of the agenda for many people in our society.

Responsibility can provide *common ground* for ethicists from different religious traditions, as I suggested at the end of the last chapter. H. Richard Niebuhr, quoted earlier, was the first one to show that this approach to ethics can stand on its own alongside other philosophical traditions. Since then, his work has influenced both Protestant and Catholic ethicists. For example, the prolific Roman Catholic author Charles Curran has adopted a "relationality-responsibility model" that "views the moral life primarily in terms of the person's multiple relationships with God, neighbor, world, and self and the subject's actions in this context."[6] God confronts us in all the choices we have to make and in all of our relationships. Therefore, our moral life is a response to the God who created us and who is the source of all values.

William Spohn, a Jesuit, has written about the use of Bible by contemporary theologians and ethicists. He calls his own view "Scripture as a Basis for Responding Love." Our experience confirms the love of God that we read about in the Bible. "The love which is the central norm for the Christian life is not an abstract principle but a specific type of experience. It is the experience of God's distinctive way of loving as manifested in the history of Jesus Christ and continued through his Spirit in the believing community."[7] He focuses much more than H. Richard Niebuhr on Jesus Christ as the object and the origin of our affections.

Albert Jonsen, whom we cited earlier, is another Jesuit who has described the use of the term "responsibility" in several recent authors, both Protestant and Catholic. In his conclusion, he looks at responsibility in relation to three areas: other moral principles or norms, which are subordinate; values; and the moral self. "The ethic of responsibility accepts and re-affirms the centrality of God the creator as a basic ethical affirmation."[8] This in turn leads us to affirm the value of the world God has created.

To summarize quickly what this all means, we can say first of all that *God is the source of all values*. The different patterns of moral reflection in the Bible teach us what values to look for in our own world. Above all else, the vision of human community found in Scripture teaches us what God values and wants from us. Second, in our life as moral agents, *we must learn to respond to what God is doing in our world*. Once again, the Bible can make us sensitive to human needs. It teaches us to look for new opportunities for service. Third, *love becomes the norm for our lives if we are to act responsibly*. As we wrestle with difficult moral issues, we will use other moral norms as well. For example, are we treating others fairly? Are we treating them as equals in God's sight? Are we respecting their God-given freedom? All of those questions are part of the larger one: Are we acting responsibly?

Exercise 38

In exercise 3, one of the questions was "Is the Bible helpful to you in deciding how you should live as a Christian? If not, why not? If so, how do you use it?" Think back to the answer you gave to that question. Would you answer it any differently now that you have read this book?

Appendix

This is a list of denominational offices that are responsible for developing social policy statements or other offices from which you can obtain copies of such statements.

1. Office of Urban Development, National Ministries
   American Baptist Churches, U.S.A.
   Valley Forge, PA 19482–0851

2. Department for Studies
   Commission for Church in Society
   Evangelical Lutheran Church in America
   8765 West Higgins Road
   Chicago, IL 60631–4190

3. National Association of Evangelicals
   P.O. Box 28
   Wheaton, IL 60189

4. Committee on Social Witness Policy
   Presbyterian Church (U.S.A.)
   100 Witherspoon Street, Room 3001
   Louisville, KY 40202–1396

5. Office for Church in Society
   United Church of Christ
   700 Prospect Avenue
   Cleveland, OH 44115

6. The General Board of Church and Society
   The United Methodist Church
   100 Maryland Avenue, N.E.
   Washington, DC 20002

7. United States Catholic Conference
   Publishing Services
   3211 Fourth Street, N.E.
   Washington, DC 20017–1194

Notes

Chapter 1

1. G. Ernest Wright and Reginald H. Fuller, *The Book of the Acts of God* (London: Gerald Duckworth & Co., 1960), p. 18.

2. Ibid., p. 20.

3. In *Baptists and the Bible* (Chicago: Moody Press, 1980), p. 401, L. Russ Bush and Tom J. Nettles make the following distinction: "Whereas 'infallible' in a general sense has referred primarily to the doctrinal content of Scripture, 'without error' has been more directly applied to the factual character of Scripture."

4. See C. Freeman Sleeper, *Black Power and Christian Responsibility* (Nashville: Abingdon Press, 1969).

5. Elizabeth Schussler Fiorenza, *Bread Not Stone* (Boston: Beacon Press, 1984), p. xvii.

6. The most complete statement of Niebuhr's views is found in his Gifford lectures, *The Nature and Destiny of Man* (New York: Scribner's, 1953).

7. See, for example, Walter Rauschenbusch, *Christianizing the Social Order* (New York: Macmillan Publishing Co., 1912).

Chapter 2

1. Seymour M. Lipset, *The First New Nation* (New York: W. W. Norton & Co., 1979).

2. Several commentators see a shift or development in Paul's argument on this point. In Galatians, Paul seems to say that the Law

was given by angels and not directly by God, so that its effect was to lead people into sinful behavior. "Development" is a modern idea. We should simply see if Paul is addressing different audiences and different circumstances in each letter.

3. The most detailed description of the situation in these letters is found in Raymond Brown, *The Community of the Beloved Disciple* (New York: Paulist Press, 1979).

Chapter 3

1. R. E. Clements, *Prophecy and Covenant*, Studies in Biblical Theology, vol. 43 (Naperville, Ill.: Alec R. Allenson, 1965), p. 26.

2. David Aune gives a detailed analysis of the forms of prophetic speech in *Prophecy in Early Christianity and the Ancient Mediterranean World* (Grand Rapids, Mich.: Wm. B. Eerdmans, 1983), pp. 88–101.

3. James L. Crenshaw, *Prophetic Conflict* (Berlin: Walter de Gruyter, 1971), especially pp. 48–61.

4. Burke O. Long, "Prophetic Authority as Social Reality," in *Canon and Authority*, ed. George W. Coats and Burke O. Long (Philadelphia: Fortress Press, 1971), p. 19.

5. The parallel in Luke 16:16 omits the second part of the verse and instead declares that after John the Baptist "the good news of the kingdom of God is proclaimed, and everyone enters it by force." In John's Gospel, the Baptist plays a quite different role. He explicitly denies that he is Elijah or "the prophet" (1:21), but instead he is the first witness to Jesus as "the one who comes" after me, the Lamb of God.

6. This passage marks a turning point in Mark's Gospel. Prior to this, Jesus tries to keep his identity secret; after this he tries to prepare his disciples for his coming death, but the disciples misunderstand him. Peter's confession that he is the Messiah represents a new level of insight, but Jesus rejects that view in favor of his identity as the Son of Man.

7. Ernst Kaesemann, in "Sentences of Holy Law in the New Testament," suggested that the earliest form of Christian law originated with prophets. His thesis has been challenged and modified, but there is evidence to support it. His essay appears in *New Testament Questions of Today*, trans. W. J. Montague (Philadelphia: Fortress Press, 1969), pp. 66–81.

8. M. Eugene Boring, *Sayings of the Risen Jesus* (Cambridge: Cambridge University Press, 1982), explores the role of Christian prophets and examines the way in which they may have influenced the sayings of Jesus.

9. David Hill, *New Testament Prophecy* (Atlanta: John Knox Press, 1979), p. 50.

Notes

Chapter 4

1. John J. Collins edited "Apocalypse: The Morphology of a Genre," *Semeia* 14 (1979). This reports on work by a group of biblical scholars. His introduction, pp. 1–19, discusses the problem of defining this literature and also points out some of its characteristics.

2. Paul D. Hanson, *The Dawn of Apocalyptic* (Cambridge, Mass.: Harvard University Press, 1979), develops this argument in great detail through a study of Old Testament texts.

3. In other Ancient Near Eastern cultures, a goddess or a gigantic sea creature represented chaos. Echoes of this myth can be seen in the opening verses of Genesis, where God creates by subduing the waters, which were "without form and void." Isaiah 51:9–10 names the dragon as Rahab; here the idea of creation is brilliantly linked with the Exodus. It is also possible that Leviathan, mentioned in Job 41:1, is a reference to this mythical figure.

4. John J. Collins, *The Apocalyptic Imagination* (New York: Crossroad, 1987), p. 89.

5. This Greek word really means "presence" or "arrival." The New Testament never speaks of Jesus' "second coming."

6. Wolfgang Schrage, *The Ethics of the New Testament,* trans. David E. Green (Philadelphia: Westminster Press, 1988), p. 341.

7. Eating food that had been sacrificed to one of the gods or goddesses "approved" by the Roman government was a difficult issue, since this included most of the meat sold in the markets. In 1 Corinthians 8–11, Paul dealt with this and related issues.

8. David Aune, "The Social Matrix of the Apocalypse of John," *Biblical Research* 26 (1981): 28.

Chapter 5

1. R. N. Whybray, *Wisdom in Proverbs,* Studies in Biblical Theology, vol. 45 (Naperville, Ill.: Alec R. Allenson, 1965), p. 14.

2. This speculation is developed even further in Sirach 1:1–10 and especially in chapter 24, where wisdom is explicitly identified with the Torah. What began as a universal principle of reason is now identified with the exclusive domain of the priests, or at least of Israel; but that development is not our main concern.

Chapter 6

1. The church has finally begun to address the issue of domestic abuse. Not much of the literature deals with a biblical point of view except to refute the claim that women must submit to their husbands,

whatever the cost in pain and suffering. One article is Susan B. Thistlethwaite, "Every Two Minutes: Battered Women and Feminist Interpretation," in *Feminist Interpretation of the Bible*, ed. Letty M. Russell (Philadelphia: Westminster Press, 1985), pp. 96–107. Two recent books are Joy M. K. Bussert, *Battered Women* (Division of Mission in North America of the Lutheran Church in America, 1986), and *Battered into Submission*, by James and Phyllis Alsdurf (Downer's Grove, Ill.: Intervarsity Press, 1989).

2. Ward Ewing, *The Power of the Lamb* (Cambridge, Mass.: Cowley Publications, 1990).

3. Stanley Hauerwas, *A Community of Character* (Notre Dame, Ind.: University of Notre Dame Press, 1981). The first chapter, pp. 9–35, is entitled "A Story-Formed Community." His thesis is developed in a number of other volumes. Unfortunately, he does not really spell out the content of the biblical story.

4. John Howard Yoder, "Kingdom as Social Ethic," in *The Priestly Kingdom* (Notre Dame, Ind.: University of Notre Dame Press, 1984), p. 92.

Chapter 7

1. Robert Benne, "The Church and Politics: Four Possible Connections," *This World* 25 (Spring 1989): 26–37.

2. Ibid., 32.

3. The result of this study appeared as an article, "The Use of Scripture in Church Social Policy Statements," in *Theology and Public Policy* 2, no. 2 (Fall 1990): 47–60.

4. American Baptist Resolution "On Citizen Responsibility in the Political Process" (Valley Forge, Pa.: American Baptist Churches, U.S.A., 1982), p. 1.

5. *The Church in Society*, a first draft of a position paper prepared by the Department of Studies of the Commission for Church in Society of the Evangelical Lutheran Church in America (Chicago: Commission for Church in Society, 1989), p. 17.

6. *The Book of Resolutions of the United Methodist Church* (Nashville: The United Methodist Publishing House, 1988), p. 15.

7. Task Force on Why and How the Church Makes a Social Policy Statement, *Why and How the Church Makes a Social Policy Statement* (Louisville, Ky.: Committee on Social Witness Policy, Presbyterian Church (U.S.A.), n.d.), p. 21.

8. *The United Church of Christ Social Policy: The First 25 Years (1957–81)*, ed. Jay Lintner (New York: The Office for Church in Society of the United Church of Christ, 1981), p. ii.

Notes

9. *NAE Resolutions* (Wheaton, Ill.: National Association of Evangelicals, 1988, second printing), p. 7.

10. *The Challenge of Peace* is available in several versions. It is included, along with articles commenting on it, in *Catholics and Nuclear War*, ed. Philip J. Murnion (New York: Crossroad, 1983). The quotation is from "Summary," found on p. 249.

11. American Baptist Churches, "Policy Statement on Church and State" (Valley Forge, Pa.: American Baptist Churches, U.S.A., 1986), p. 6.

12. *Why and How the Church Makes Social Witness Policy*, p. 17.

Chapter 8

1. Jonathan Schell, *The Fate of the Earth* (New York: Alfred A. Knopf, 1982), p. 113.

2. Quoted by Joseph Adelson and Chester E. Finn, Jr., "Terrorizing Children," in *Commentary* 79 (April 1985): 29.

3. Roland H. Bainton, *Christian Attitudes toward War and Peace* (New York: Abingdon Press, 1960), pp. 53–54. For a more detailed study of Jesus' command, see Victor Paul Furnish, *The Love Commandment in the New Testament* (Nashville: Abingdon Press, 1972); Reginald H. and Ilsa Fuller, trans., *Essays on the Love Commandment* (Philadelphia: Fortress Press, 1978); and Pheme Perkins, *Love Commands in the New Testament* (New York: Paulist Press, 1982).

4. John Howard Yoder, *The Politics of Jesus* (Grand Rapids, Mich.: Wm. B. Eerdmans, 1972).

5. Richard Horsley, *Jesus and the Spiral of Violence* (San Francisco: Harper & Row, 1987).

6. John H. Elliott has demonstrated this brilliantly in his discussion of 1 Peter, entitled *A Home for the Homeless* (Philadelphia: Fortress Press, 1981).

7. In his otherwise excellent commentary *Revelation* in the Interpretation commentary series (Louisville: John Knox Press, 1989), M. Eugene Boring argues that all of this language is metaphor. That of course tones down the militaristic imagery, but we face the same question that we did with the "holy war" position. How much of this is meant to be taken seriously?

8. Bainton, *Christian Attitudes toward War and Peace*, p. 143.

9. Joseph L. Allen, *Love and Conflict* (Nashville: Abingdon Press, 1984), p. 188.

10. The United Methodist Council of Bishops, *In Defense of Creation: The Nuclear Crisis and a Just Peace*, Foundation Document (Nashville: Graded Press, 1986), pp. 33–34. Quotation is used by permission of Graded Press.

11. See, for example, Robert Heyer, ed., *Nuclear Disarmament* (New York: Paulist Press, 1982) and Donald L. Davidson, *Nuclear Weapons and the American Churches* (Boulder, Colo.: Westview Press, 1983).

12. "Christian Obedience in a Nuclear Age," *Church and Society* 78 (July/August 1988): 15.

13. *The Challenge to Peace* (Washington, D.C.: National Conference of Catholic Bishops/United States Catholic Conference, 1983).

14. Charles Curran, "The Moral Methodology of the Bishops' Pastoral," in *Catholics and Nuclear War*, ed. Philip Murnion (New York: Crossroad, 1983), pp. 47–48. In the same volume, Sandra Schneiders criticizes "the failure to integrate the biblical material into the central reasoning of the document" (p. 91); but she really wants to substitute an entirely different method for interpreting the New Testament, using Jesus' example of "ultimate self-sacrifice" as the basis for a pacifist ethic.

15. *"Guidelines" for Peace, Freedom and Security Studies* (Wheaton, Ill.: National Association of Evangelicals, 1986).

Chapter 9

1. To give one example of this debate, the Presbyterian Church (U.S.A.) published a "National Dialogue on Abortion Perspectives" in *Church and Society* 80 (January/February 1990).

2. Cited in J. Gordon Melton, *Churches Speak on: Abortion* (Detroit: Gale Research Inc., 1989), p. 29.

3. See Melton, *Churches Speak on: Abortion*.

4. Daniel J. Callahan, *Abortion: Law, Choice and Morality* (New York: Macmillan Publishing Co., 1970), p. 410. The most detailed historical treatment of the Catholic position is found in John T. Noonan, Jr., *Contraception: A History of Its Treatment by Catholic Theologians and Canonists* (Cambridge, Mass.: Harvard University Press, 1966). A somewhat different reading is given in John R. Connery, *Abortion: The Development of the Roman Catholic Perspective* (Chicago: Loyola University Press, 1977).

5. Roy J. Enquist, "The Churches' Response to Abortion," *Word and World* 5 (1985): 414–25.

6. Ibid., p. 131.

7. Excerpts from 1969 and 1985 letters by the bishops are found in *The Churches Speak on: Abortion*, pp. 6f. and 16f.

8. Stanley Hauerwas, "Abortion: The Agent's Perspective," pp. 147–65 in *Vision and Virtue* (Notre Dame, Ind.: Fides Publishers, 1974; Notre Dame, Ind.: University of Notre Dame Press, 1981), p. 152.

Notes

9. Stanley Hauerwas, "Why Abortion Is a Religious Issue," pp. 196–211 in *A Community of Character* (Notre Dame, Ind.: University of Notre Dame Press, 1981), p. 198. Also in the same volume is a chapter "Abortion: Why the Arguments Fail," pp. 212–29.

10. Beverly Wildung Harrison, *Our Right to Choose* (Boston: Beacon Press, 1983), p. 199.

11. Mark Olson, "Back to the Bible," *The Other Side* (June 1980): 34; see also pp. 34–44.

12. This is especially true of those Roman Catholic and other interpreters who base their views on the Greek translation of verse 22, reading the fetus as being "formed" and having life in the full sense.

13. "The Value of Human Life," a statement received as information by the Eighth General Convention of The American Lutheran Church and published in a collection of statements titled *Abortion* (Minneapolis, Minn.: Office of Church and Society, n.d.).

14. *Abortion*, one of three statements approved by the board of the Commission for Church in Society (Chicago: Evangelical Lutheran Church in America, 1991).

15. This quote is contained in an article by Johnny Greene, "The Astonishing Wrongs of the New Moral Right," in *Playboy* (January 1981): 118.

16. Frank Morris, "No Moral Arguments Against Destroying Abortuaries," *The Wanderer* (August 1, 1985); reprinted in *Abortion: Opposing Viewpoints*, ed. Bonnie Szumski (San Diego, Calif.: Greenhaven Press, 1986), pp. 181–84.

Chapter 10

1. For an illustration of this point, see Willard M. Swartley, *Slavery, Sabbath, War, and Women* (Scottdale, Pa.: Herald Press, 1983).

2. See C. Freeman Sleeper, *Black Power and Christian Responsibility* (Nashville: Abingdon Press, 1969).

3. H. Richard Niebuhr, *The Responsible Self* (New York: Harper & Row, 1963), p. 126.

4. Albert R. Jonsen, S.J., *Responsibility in Modern Religious Ethics* (Washington: Corpus Books, 1968).

5. Ann Blackman, Tom Currey, and Edwin M. Reingold, "Crybabies: Eternal Victims," *Time* (August 12, 1991): 18.

6. Charles E. Curran, *Moral Theology: A Continuing Journey* (Notre Dame, Ind.: University of Notre Dame Press, 1982), p. 44. His article "The Role and Function of the Scriptures in Moral Theology" is very close to the position that I have argued in this book; it is reprinted in *Readings in Moral Theology #4: The Use of Scripture in Moral Theology,*

ed. Charles E. Curran and Richard A. McCormick, S.J. (New York: Paulist Press, 1984), pp. 178–212.

7. William C. Spohn, S.J., *What Are They Saying about Scripture and Ethics?* (New York: Paulist Press, 1984). Chapter 6 is found on pp. 106–28; the quotation is from p. 106.

8. Jonsen, *Responsibility in Modern Religious Ethics*, p. 215.

Bibliography

This short bibliography lists no articles, although the journal *Interpretation* regularly touches on these issues. The books listed do not use foreign languages and should be readily available at a religious bookstore or an undergraduate library. This list does not include works cited in the notes.

Chapter 1

The Authority of Scripture

Achtemeier, Paul J. *The Inspiration of Scripture: Problems and Proposals.* Philadelphia: Fortress Press, 1980.

Countryman, William. *Biblical Authority or Biblical Tyrrany?* Philadelphia: Fortress Press, 1981.

Pinnock, Clark H. *The Scripture Principle.* San Francisco: Harper & Row, 1984.

Interpreting Scripture

Alter, Robert, and Kermode, Frank, eds. *The Literary Guide to the Bible.* Cambridge, Mass.: Belknap Press, 1987.

Scripture and Ethics

Birch, Bruce C., and Rasmussen, Larry L. *Bible and Ethics in the Christian Life.* Revised and expanded. Minneapolis: Augsburg Press, 1989.

BIBLIOGRAPHY

Daly, Robert J., S.J., ed. *Christian Biblical Ethics*. New York: Paulist Press, 1984.

Everding, H. Edward, and Wilbanks, Dana W. *Decision Making and the Bible*. Valley Forge, Pa.: Judson Press, 1975.

Longnecker, Richard N. *New Testament Social Ethics for Today*. Grand Rapids, Mich.: Wm. B. Eerdmans, 1984.

General Surveys

Efird, James M. *How to Interpret the Bible*. Atlanta: John Knox Press, 1984.

————. *These Things Are Written*. Atlanta: John Knox Press, 1978.

Muilenberg, James. *The Way of Israel*. Harper Torchbook. New York: Harper & Row, 1961.

Sanders, James A. *Torah and Canon*. Philadelphia: Fortress Press, 1972.

Chapter 2

Blenkinsopp, Joseph. *Wisdom and Law in the Old Testament*. The Oxford Bible Series. Oxford: Oxford University Press, 1983.

Patrick, Dale. *Old Testament Law*. Atlanta: John Knox Press, 1985.

Sanders, E. P. *Paul, the Law and the Jewish People*. Philadelphia: Fortress Press, 1983.

Ziesler, John. *Pauline Christianity*. The Oxford Bible Series. Oxford: Oxford University Press, 1983.

Chapter 3

Blenkinsopp, Joseph. *A History of Prophecy in Israel*. Philadelphia: Westminster Press, 1983.

Brueggemann, Walter. *The Prophetic Imagination*. Philadelphia: Fortress Press, 1978.

Heschel, Abraham. *The Prophets*. New York: Harper & Row, 1963.

Reid, David P., SS.CC. *What Are They Saying about the Prophets*? New York: Paulist Press, 1980.

Wilson, Robert R. *Prophecy and Society in Ancient Israel*. Philadelphia: Fortress Press, 1980.

Chapter 4

Russell, D. S. *The Method and Message of Jewish Apocalyptic*. Philadelphia: Westminster Press, 1964.

Chapter 5

Crenshaw, James L. *Old Testament Wisdom: An Introduction*. Atlanta: John Knox Press, 1981.

Bibliography

Morgan, Donn F. *Wisdom in the Old Testament Traditions*. Atlanta: John Knox Press, 1981.

Murphy, Roland E., O.Carm. *Wisdom Literature and Psalms*. Interpreting Biblical Texts. Nashville: Abingdon Press, 1983.

Wilken, Robert L. *Aspects of Wisdom in Judaism and Early Christianity*. Notre Dame, Ind.: University of Notre Dame Press, 1975.

Chapter 6

Furnish, Victor Paul. *The Moral Teaching of Paul*. Nashville: Abingdon Press, 1979.

————.*Theology and Ethics in Paul*. Nashville: Abingdon Press, 1968.

Gerhardsson, Birger. *The Ethos of the Bible*. Translated by Stephen Westerholm. Philadelphia: Fortress Press, 1979.

Maynard-Reid, Pedrito U. *Poverty and Wealth in James*. Maryknoll, N.Y.: Orbis Books, 1987.

Chapter 9

Callahan, Sidney, and Callahan, Daniel, eds. *Abortion: Understanding Differences*. New York: Plenum Press, 1984.

Harrison, Beverly Wildung. *Our Right to Choose*. Boston: Beacon Press, 1983.

Hull, Gretchen Gaebelein. *Applying the Scriptures*. Grand Rapids, Mich.: Zondervan Publishing House, 1987.

Chapter 10

Johnson, Luke T. *Decision-Making in the Church*. Philadelphia: Fortress Press, 1983.

Mott, Stephen Charles. *Biblical Ethics and Social Change*. New York: Oxford University Press, 1982.

Ogletree, Thomas W. *The Use of the Bible in Christian Ethics*. Philadelphia: Fortress Press, 1983.

Verhey, Allen. *The Great Reversal*. Grand Rapids, Mich.: Wm. B. Eerdmans, 1984.